Old English Charms, Poems, and Proverbs 1

Original Texts, Translations, and Word Lists

Translated by Matthew Leigh Embleton

Copyright ©2025 Matthew Leigh Embleton. All rights reserved.

Old English Charms, Poems, and Proverbs 1

1. A Proverb from Winfrid's Time 5
2. The Gloria II 6
3. Bede's Death Song (Northumbrian Version) 7
4. Bede's Death Song (The Hague Version) 9
5. Bede's Death Song (West Saxon Version) 11
6. Latin-English Proverbs 13
7. The Brussels Cross 15
8. Caedmon's Hymn (Northumbrian Version) 17
9. Caedmon's Hymn (West Saxon Version) 19
10. Pharaoh 21
11. Alms-Giving 23
12. Capture of the Five Boroughs 25
13. Thureth 27
14. The Lord's Prayer I 29
15. Charm 8 For a Swarm of Bees 32
16. Charm 12 Against a Wen 34
17. The Partridge 36
18. Aldhelm 39
19. Homiletic Fragment II 42
20. Charm 10 For Loss of Cattle 45
21. Charm 7 For the Water-Elf Disease 48
22. Wulf and Eadwacer 51
23. The Coronation of Edgar 54
24. Durham 57
25. Charm 5 For Loss of Cattle 60
26. Charm 9 For Loss of Cattle 63
27. Charm 3 Against a Dwarf 66
28. A Summons to Prayer 69
29. The Death of Edward 73
30. Waldere B 77
31. Waldere A 81
32. The Death of Alfred 86

Word List *(Ænglisc to English)* 90
Word List *(English to Ænglisc)* 109

Cover: Old English text over an outline of England. Author's design.

The original Old English texts are in the public domain.
These translations ©2021 Matthew Leigh Embleton
©2025 Matthew Leigh Embleton (This Edition)

Acknowledgments

I have long been fascinated by languages and history, and I am very grateful to the special people in my life who have supported and encouraged me in my work. Thank you for believing in me. You know who you are.

Introduction

Old English (Ænglisc) is the earliest recorded form of the English language. It was brought to Britain by Anglo-Saxon settlers in the mid-5th century. The first literary works in Old English date from the mid 7th century. Spelling was not standardised but varied by region and dialect over time.

Contained in this book:
A Proverb from Winfrid's Time, The Gloria II, Bede's Death Song (Northumbrian Version), Bede's Death Song (The Hague Version), Bede's Death Song (West Saxon Version), Latin-English Proverbs, The Brussels Cross, Caedmon's Hymn (Northumbrian Version), Caedmon's Hymn (West Saxon Version), Pharaoh, Alms-Giving, The Capture of the Five Boroughs, Thureth, The Lord's Prayer I, Charm 8 For a Swarm of Bees, Charm 12 Against a Wen, The Partridge, Aldhelm, Homiletic Fragment II, Charm 10 For Loss of Cattle, Charm 7 For the Water-Elf Disease, Wulf and Eadwacer, The Coronation of Edgar, Durham, Charm 5 For Loss of Cattle, Charm 9 For Loss of Cattle, Charm 3 Against a Dwarf, A Summons to Prayer, The Death of Edward, Waldere B, Waldere A, The Death of Alfred

The texts are presented in their original Old English, with a literal word-for-word line-by-line translation, and a Modern English translation, all side-by-side. In this way, it is possible to see and feel how Old English worked and how it has evolved. Also included are individual word lists for each text, and an overall word list.

This book is designed to be of use and interest to anyone with a passion for the Old English language, Anglo-Saxon history, or languages and history in general.

1 A Proverb from Winfrid's Time

Ænglisc	Literal	English

1 Oft daed lata
    domę forędit,
	Often deed slack
	    delay glory,
		Often the slack of deed
		    delay seeking glory,

2 sigisiþa gahwem,
    swyltit þi ana.
	victorious undertaking,
	    die therefore alone.
		in each victorious undertaking,
		    and die therefore alone.

Word List

Ænglisc	English
A, a	
ana	alone
D, d	
daed	deed
domę	glory
F, f	
forędit	delays
G, g	
gahwem	undertaking
L, l	
lata	slack
O, o	
oft	often
S, s	
sigisiþa	successful
swyltit	dies
Þ, þ	
þi	therefore

2 The Gloria II

	Ænglisc	Literal	English
1	Wuldor sy ðe and wurðmynt, wereda drihten,	Glory be to-thee and honour, army lord,	Glory be to thee and honour, lord of armies,
2	fæder on foldan, fægere gemæne,	father on earth, good universal,	father on earth, the universal good,
3	mid sylfan sunu and soðum gaste.	with his-self son and true spirit.	with his own son and the true spirit.
4	Amen.	Amen.	Amen.

Word List

Ænglisc	English	Ænglisc	English
A, a		on	on
amen	amen	S, s	
and	and	soðum	true
D, d		sunu	son
drihten	lord	sy	be
		sylfan	his-self
Ð, ð		W, w	
ðe	to-thee	wereda	army
		wuldor	glory
F, f		wurðmynt	honour
fæder	father		
fægere	good		
foldan	earth		
G, g			
gaste	spirit		
gemæne	universal		
M, m			
mid	with		
O, o			

3 Bede's Death Song (Northumbrian Version)

	Ænglisc	Literal	English
1	Fore þaem neidfaerae naenig wiurðit	For the needed-journey none will-be	For the necessary journey no one will be
2	þoncsnotturra, þan him þarf sie	thought-wiser, than he needs to-be	wiser in thought than he needs to be
3	to ymbhycggannae aer his hiniongae	to about-think before he from-here-goes	to consider before he goes from here
4	huaet his gastae godaes aeðða yflaes	what-of his spirit good or evil	what of his spirit is good or evil
5	aefter deoðdaege doemid weorðae.	after death-day deemed of-worth.	after his death day will be judged of its worth.

Word List

Ænglisc	English	Ænglisc	English
A, a			
		N, n	
aeðða	or		
aefter	after	naenig	none
aer	before	neidfaerae	needed-journey
D, d		**S, s**	
deoðdaege	death-day	sie	to-be
doemid	deemed		
		T, t	
F, f			
		to	to
fore	for		
		Þ, þ	
G, g			
		þaem	the
gastae	spirit	þan	than
godaes	good	þarf	needs
		þoncsnotturra	thought-wiser
H, h			
		W, w	
him	he		
hiniongae	from-here-goes	weorðae	of-worth
his	he, his	wiurðit	will-be
huaet	what-of		

Old English Charms, Poems, and Proverbs 1

Bede's Death Song
(Northumbrian Version)

Ænglisc   English

Y, y

yflaes   evil
ymbhycggannae   about-think

4 Bede's Death Song (The Hague Version)

	Ænglisc	Literal	English

1	Fore ðaem nedfere
	    nenig wiorðeð
		For the needed-journey
		    none will-be
			For the necessary journey
			    no one will be

2	ðonosnottorra
	    ðon him ðearf siae
		thought-wiser
		    than he needs to-be
			wiser in thought
			    than he needs to be

3	to ymbhycgenne
	    aer his hinionge
		to about-think
		    before he from-here-goes
			to consider
			    before he goes from here

4	hwet his gastæ
	    godes oððe yfles
		what-of his spirit
		    good or evil
			what of his spirit
			    is good or evil

5	efter deaðdege
	    doemed wiorðe.
		after death-day
		    deemed of-worth.
			after his death day
			    will be judged of its worth.

Word List

Ænglisc	English	Ænglisc	English
A, a		gastæ	spirit
aer	before	godes	good
		H, h	
D, d			
deaðdege	death-day	him	he
doemed	deemed	hinionge	from-here-goes
		his	he, his
Ð, ð		hwet	what-of
ðaem	the	**N, n**	
ðearf	needs		
ðon	than	nedfere	needed-journey
ðonosnottorra	thought-wiser	nenig	none
		O, o	
E, e			
efter	after	oððe	or
		S, s	
F, f			
fore	for	siae	to-be
		T, t	
G, g			
		to	to

Ænglisc	English
W, w	
wiorðe.	of-worth
wiorðeð	will-be
Y, y	
yfles	evil
ymbhycgenne	about-think

5 Bede's Death Song (West Saxon Version)

Ænglisc	Literal	English

1 For þam nedfere
    næni wyrþeþ
	For the needed-journey
	    none will-be
		For the necessary journey
		    no one will be

2 þances snotera,
    þonne him þearf sy
	thought wiser,
	    than he needs to-be
		wiser in thought
		    than he needs to be

3 to gehicgenne
    ær his heonengange
	to think
	    before he from-here-goes
		to consider
		    before he goes from here

4 hwæt his gaste
    godes oþþe yfeles
	what-of his spirit
	    good or evil
		what of his spirit
		    is good or evil

5 æfter deaþe heonon
    demed weorþe.
	after death from-here
	    deemed of-worth.
		after his death day
		    will be judged of its worth.

Word List

Ænglisc	English	Ænglisc	English
Æ, æ		hwæt	what-of
æfter	after	**N, n**	
ær	before		
		næni	none
D, d		nedfere	needed-journey
deaþe	death	**O, o**	
demed	deemed		
		oþþe	or
F, f			
		S, s	
for	for		
		snotera	wiser
G, g		sy	to-be
gaste	spirit	**T, t**	
gehicgenne	think		
godes	good	to	to
H, h		**Þ, þ**	
heonengange	from-here-goes	þam	the
heonon	from-here	þances	thought
him	he	þearf	needs
his	he, his	þonne	than

Ænglisc	English
W, w	
weorþe	of-worth
wyrþeþ	will-be
Y, y	
yfeles	evil

6 Latin-English Proverbs

	Ænglisc	Literal	English

1	*Ardor frigesscit,*
	    nitor squalescit,
		Heat grows-cold,
		    shining grows-dirty,
			Heat grows cold,
			    that which shines grows dirty,

2	*amor abolescit,*
	    lux obtenebrescit.
		love fades-away,
		    light grows-dark.
			love fades away,
			    light grows dark.

3	*Hat acolað,*
	    hwit asolað,
		Heat grows-cold,
		    white grows-dirty,
			Heat grows cold,
			    that which is white grows dirty,

4	*leof alaðaþ,*
	
	    leoht aðystrað.
		love becomes-loathed,
		
		    light grows-dark.
			that which is loved becomes loathed,
			    light grows dark

5	*Senescunt omnia*
	    que æterna non sunt.
		Grows-old everything
		    which eternal not they-are.
			Everything grows old
			    of which they are not eternal.

6	*æghwæt forealdað*
	    þæs þe ece ne byð.
		Everything grows-old
		    that which eternal not be.
			Everything grows old
			    that is not eternal.

Word List

Ænglisc	English	Ænglisc	English
A, a			
abolescit	fades-away (Latin)	**F, f**	
acolað	grows-cold	*forealdað*	grows-old
aðystrað	grows-dark	*frigesscit*	grows-cold (Latin)
alaðaþ	becomes-loathed		
amor	love (Latin)	**H, h**	
ardor	heat (Latin)		
asolað	grows-dirty	*hat*	heat
		hwit	white
Æ, æ			
		L, l	
æghwæt	everything		
æterna	eternal (Latin)	*leof*	love
		leoht	light
B, b		*lux*	light (Latin)
byð	be	**N, n**	
E, e		*ne*	not
		nitor	shining (Latin)
ece	eternal	*non*	not (Latin)

Ænglisc English

O, o

obtenebrescit grows-dark (Latin)
omnia everything (Latin)

Q, q

que which (Latin)

S, s

senescunt grows-old (Latin)
squalescit grows-dirty (Latin)
sunt they-are (Latin)

Þ, þ

þæs that
þe which

7 The Brussels Cross

Ænglisc	Literal	English
1 Rod is min nama.	Cross is my name.	Cross is my name.
Geo ic ricne cyning	Once I a-powerful king	Once, a powerful king I
2 bær byfigynde,	bore trembling,	bore trembling,
blode bestemed.	bloodied wet.	bloodied wet.
3 þas rode het æþlmær wyrican	This cross commanded Æthelmaer made	this cross Æthelmaer commanded made
and Aðelwold hys beroþor	and Æthelwold his brother	and Æthelwold his brother
4 Criste to lofe for ælfrices	Christ for love because-of	for the love of Christ and for
saule hyra beroþor.	Ælfric's soul their brother.	Ælfric's soul, their brother.

Word List

Ænglisc	English
A, a	
Aðelwold	Æthelwold (a name)
and	and
Æ, æ	
Ælfrices	Ælfric's (a name)
Æþlmær	Æthelmaer (a name)
B, b	
bær	bore
beroþor	brother
bestemed	wet
blode	bloodied
byfigynde	trembling
C, c	
Criste	Christ (a name)
cyning	king
F, f	
for	because-of
G, g	
Geo	once
H, h	
het	commanded
hyra	their
hys	his
I, i	
ic	I
is	is
L, l	
lofe	love
M, m	
min	my
N, n	
nama	name
R, r	

Ænglisc	English
ricne	a-powerful
Rod	cross
rode	cross
S, s	
saule	soul
T, t	
to	for
Þ, þ	
þas	this
W, w	
wyrican	made

8 Caedmon's Hymn (Northumbrian Version)

	Ænglisc	Literal	English

1	Nu scylun hergan
	    hefaenricaes uard,
		Now shall-we honour
		    heaven-kingdom's ward,
			Now shall we honour
			    the guardian of heaven,

2	metudæs maecti
	    end his modgidanc,
		the-measurer's might
		    and his mind-plans,
			the measurer's might
			    and his mind's design,

3	uerc uuldurfadur,
	    sue he uundra gihuaes,
		work-of glory-father,
		    as he wonder each,
			the work of the glorious father,
			    as he of each wonder

4	eci dryctin,
	    or astelidæ.
		eternal lord,
		    origin established.
			eternal lord,
			    the origin established.

5	He aerist scop
	    aelda barnum
		He first created
		    elders' children
			He first created
			    for the children of elders

6	heben til hrofe,
	    haleg scepen;
		heaven for a-roof,
		    holy shaper;
			heaven for a roof,
			    holy shaper;

7	tha middungeard
	    moncynnæs uard,
		then middle-earth
		    mankind's ward,
			then middle-earth
			    mankind's guardian

8	eci dryctin,
	    æfter tiadæ
		eternal lord,
		    after titled
			eternal lord,
			    after titled

9	firum foldu,
	    frea allmectig.
		for-men lands,
		    lord almighty.
			the lands for men,
			    lord almighty.

Word List

Ænglisc	English	Ænglisc	English
A, a		**E, e**	
aelda	elders'	eci	eternal
aerist	first	end	and
allmectig	almighty		
astelidæ	established	**F, f**	
		firum	for-men
Æ, æ		foldu	lands
æfter	after	frea	lord
B, b		**G, g**	
barnum	children	gihuaes	each
D, d		**H, h**	
dryctin	lord		

Ænglisc	English
haleg	holy
he	he
heben	heaven
hefaenricaes	heaven-kingdom's
hergan	honour
his	his
hrofe	a-roof

M, m

maecti	might
metudæs	the-measurer's
middungeard	middle-earth
modgidanc	mind-plans
moncynnæs	mankind's

N, n

Nu	now

O, o

or	origin

S, s

scepen	shaper
scop	created
scylun	shall-we
sue	as

T, t

tha	then
tiadæ	titled
til	for

U, u

uard	ward
uerc	work-of
uuldurfadur	glory-father
uundra	wonder

9 Caedmon's Hymn (West Saxon Version)

Ænglisc	Literal	English
1 Nu sculon herigean 　heofonrices weard,	Now shall-we honour 　heaven-kingdom's ward,	Now shall we honour 　the guardian of heaven,
2 meotodes meahte 　and his modgeþanc,	the-measurer's might 　and his mind-plans,	the measurer's might 　and his mind's design,
3 weorc wuldorfæder, 　swa he wundra gehwæs,	work-of glory-father, 　as he wonder each,	the work of the glorious father, 　as he of each wonder
4 ece drihten, 　or onstealde.	eternal lord, 　origin established.	eternal lord, 　the origin established.
5 He ærest sceop 　eorðan bearnum	He first created 　elders' children	He first created 　for the children of elders
6 heofon to hrofe, 　halig scyppend;	heaven for a-roof, 　holy shaper;	heaven for a roof, 　holy shaper;
7 þa middangeard 　moncynnes weard,	then middle-earth 　mankind's ward,	then middle-earth 　mankind's guardian
8 ece drihten, 　æfter teode	eternal lord, 　after titled	eternal lord, 　after titled
9 firum foldan, 　frea ælmihtig.	for-men lands, 　lord almighty.	the lands for men, 　lord almighty.

Word List

Ænglisc	English
A, a	
and	and
Æ, æ	
æfter	after
ælmihtig	almighty
ærest	first
B, b	
bearnum	children
D, d	
drihten	lord
E, e	
ece	eternal
eorðan	elders'
F, f	
firum	for-men
foldan	lands
frea	lord
G, g	
gehwæs	each
H, h	
halig	holy

Ænglisc	English	Ænglisc	English
he	he	wundra	wonder
heofon	heaven		
heofonrices	heaven-kingdom's		
herigean	honour		
his	his		
hrofe	a-roof		

M, m

meahte	might
meotodes	the-measurer's
middangeard	middle-earth
modgeþanc	mind-plans
moncynnes	mankind's

N, n

Nu	now

O, o

onstealde	established
or	origin

S, s

sceop	created
sculon	shall-we
scyppend	shaper
swa	as

T, t

teode	titled
to	for

Þ, þ

þa	then

W, w

weard	ward
weorc	work-of
wuldorfæder	glory-father

10 Pharaoh

	Ænglisc	Literal	English
1	*"Saga me hwæt þær weorudes wære ealles*	"Tell me what there troops were all	"Tell me what troops there were which were all
2	*on Farones fyrde, þa hy folc godes*	in Pharoah's army, when they folk heathen-god's	in the Pharoah's army, when they the heathen-god's folk
3	*þurh feondscipe fylgan ongunn...."*	sake-of enmity pursued undertake...."	for the sake of enmity undertook to pursue…"
4	*"Nat ic hit be wihte, butan ic wene þus,*	"Not I it about anything, except I think thus,	"I do not know anythng about it, except that I think,
5	*þæt þær screoda wære gescyred rime*	that there numbered were alloted counted	that there were numbered, alloted and counted
6	*siex hun... ...a searohæbbendra;*	six hundred… …all armoured;	six hundred… …all armoured;
7	*þæt eal fornam yþ...*	that all swept-away wave…	that were swept away by a wave…
8	*wraþe wyrde in woruldrice".*	wrathfully destroyed in world-kingdom".	wrathfully destroyed in the kingdom of the world".

Word List

Ænglisc	English	Ænglisc	English
A, a		*fylgan*	pursued
a	all	*fyrde*	army
B, b		**G, g**	
be	about	*gescyred*	alloted
butan	except	*godes*	God-heathen's
E, e		**H, h**	
eal	all	*hit*	it
ealles	all	*hun*	hundred
F, f		*hwæt*	what
Farones	Pharoah's	*hy*	they
feondscipe	enmity	**I, i**	
folc	folk	*ic*	I
fornam	swept-away	*in*	in

Ænglisc	English
M, m	
me	me
N, n	
nat	not
O, o	
on	in
ongunn	undertake
R, r	
rime	counted
S, s	
saga	tell
screoda	numbered
searohæbbendra	armoured
siex	six
Þ, þ	
þa	when
þær	there
þæt	that
þurh	sake-of
þus	thus
W, w	
wære	were
wene	think
weorudes	troops
wihte	anything
woruldrice	world-kingdom
wraþe	wrathfully
wyrde	destroyed
Y, y	
yþ	wave

11 Alms-Giving

Ænglisc	Literal	English
1 Wel bið þam eorle	Well being that earl	Well will it be for the earl
þe him on innan hafað,	that he in within has,	that he has within him,
2 reþehygdig wer,	right-thinking man,	a right-thinking man,
rume heortan;	roomy heart;	a roomy heart;
3 þæt him biþ for worulde	that he be for the-world	that will be for him in the world
weorðmynda mæst,	worth-minded most,	the most worthy,
4 ond for ussum dryhtne	and for us the-lord	and before us the lord
doma selast.	deeming excellence.	of excellent judgements.
5 Efne swa he mid wætre	Even as he with water	Even as he with water
þone weallendan	then welling	then welling
6 leg adwæsce,	lays quenched,	lays quenched,
þæt he leng ne mæg	that it longer not may	that it no longer may
7 blac byrnende	bright burning	brightly burning
burgum sceððan,	cities harm,	harming cities,
8 swa he mid ælmessan	so he with alms	so he with alms
ealle toscufeð	all do-away	will do away with all
9 synna wunde,	sin wounds,	wounds of sin,
sawla lacnað.	souls healed.	and heal souls.

Word List

Ænglisc	English
A, a	
adwæsce	quenched
Æ, æ	
ælmessan	alms
B, b	
bið	being
biþ	be
blac	bright
burgum	cities
byrnende	burning
D, d	
doma	deeming
dryhtne	the-lord
E, e	
ealle	all
efne	even
eorle	earl
F, f	
for	for
H, h	
hafað	has
he	he, it
heortan	heart
him	he

Ænglisc	English	Ænglisc	English
I, i		þam	that
		þe	that
innan	within	þone	then
L, l		U, u	
lacnað	healed	ussum	us
leg	lays		
leng	longer	W, w	
M, m		wætre	water
		weallendan	welling
mæg	may	wel	well
mæst	most	weorðmynda	worth-minded
mid	with	wer	man
		worulde	the-world
N, n		wunde	wounds
ne	not		
O, o			
on	in		
ond	and		
R, r			
reþehygdig	right-thinking		
rume	roomy		
S, s			
sawla	souls		
sceððan	harm		
selast	excellence		
swa	as, so		
synna	sin		
T, t			
toscufeð	do-away		
Þ, þ			
þæt	that		

Old English Charms, Poems, and Proverbs 1

12 Capture of the Five Boroughs

	Ænglisc	Literal	English
1	Her Eadmund cyning, Engla þeoden,	Here Edmund king, English lord,	Here King Edmund, lord of the English,
2	mæcgea mundbora, Myrce geeode,	kinsmen guardian, Mercia conquered,	Guardian of kinsmen, conquered Mercia,
3	dyre dædfruma, swa Dor scadeþ,	dear deed-doer, as The Dore borders,	The dear doer of deeds, as the Dore borders it,
4	Hwitanwyllesgeat and Humbra ea,	Whitwell Gap and Humber river,	The Whitwell Fap and the River Humber,
5	brada brimstream. Burga fife,	broad ocean-stream. Boroughs five,	broad ocean-stream. Five Boroughs,
6	Ligoraceaster and Lincylene	Leicester and Lincoln	Leicester and Lincoln
7	and Snotingaham, swylce Stanford eac	and Nottingham, likewise Stamford also	and Nottingham, also Stamford
8	and Deoraby. Dæne wæran æror	and Derby. Danes were before	and Derby. Danes were previously
9	under Norðmannum nyde gebegde	under Northmen subjected bowed	under the Northmen subjected and bowed
10	on hæþenra hæfteclommum	in heathen binding-chains	in heathen binding chains
11	lange þrage, oþ hie alysde eft	long for-a-time, until he released afterwards	for a long time, until he released them afterwards
12	for his weorþscipe wiggendra hleo,	for his worthship warriors protecting,	for his worthiness protector of warriors,
13	afera Eadweardes, Eadmund cyning.	heir of Eadwcard, Eadmund king.	son of Eadweard King Edmund.

Word List

Ænglisc	English	*Ænglisc*	English
A, a		B, b	
afera	heir-of	brada	broad
alysde	released	brimstream	ocean-stream
and	and	Burga	boroughs
Æ, æ		C, c	
æror	before	cyning	king, king

Ænglisc	English	Ænglisc	English

D, d

dædfruma	deed-doer
Dæne	Danes
Deoraby	Derby
Dor	The Dore
dyre	dear

mæcgea	kinsmen
mundbora	guardian
myrce	Mercia

N, n

| Norðmannum | Northmen |
| nyde | subjected |

E, e

ea	river
eac	also
Eadmund	Eadmund, Edmund
Eadweardes	Edward
eft	afterwards
engla	English

O, o

| on | in |
| oþ | until |

S, s

scadeþ	borders
Snotingaham	Nottingham
Stanford	Stamford
swa	as
swylce	likewise

F, f

| fife | five |
| for | for |

G, g

| gebegde | bowed |
| geeode | conquered |

Þ, þ

| þeoden | lord |
| þrage | for-a-time |

H, h

hæfteclommum	binding-chains
hæþenra	heathen
her	here
hie	he
his	his
hleo	protecting
Humbra	Humber
Hwitanwyllesgeat	Whitwell Gap

U, u

| under | under |

W, w

wæran	were
weorþscipe	worthship
wiggendra	warriors

L, l

lange	long
Ligoraceaster	Leicester
Lincylene	Lincoln

M, m

13 Thureth

	Ænglisc	Literal	English

1	Ic eom halgungboc;
	    healde hine dryhten
		I am holy-book;
		    hold he the-lord
			I am of the holy book;
			    may the lord keep him

2	þe me fægere þus
	    frætewum belegde.
		that me beautifully thus
		    ornaments covered.
			that has beautifully
			    covered me in ornaments.

3	þureð to þance
	    þus het me wyrcean,
		Thureth to thank
		    thus ordered me created,
			Thureth thankfully
			    thus ordered me to be created,

4	to loue and to wurðe,
	    þam þe leoht gesceop.
		to love and to worth,
		    them that light created.
			to love and honour,
			    he who created the light.

5	Gemyndi is he
	    mihta gehwylcre
		Mindful is he
		    mighty works
			He is mindful
			    of all the mighty works

6	þæs þe he on foldan
	    gefremian mæg,
		so that he on earth
		    accomplish may,
			which he on earth
			    is able to accomplish,

7	and him geþancie
	    þeoda waldend
		and him thank
		    nations ruler
			and he shall be thanked
			    by the ruler of nations

8	þæs þe he on gemynde
	    madma manega
		so that he in mindful
		    treasures many
			because he, mindful
			    of many treasures

9	wyle gemearcian
	    metode to lace;
		wishes to-mark
		    the-Creator to offer;
			wishes to mark me
			    as an offering to the creator;

10	and he sceal æce lean
	    ealle findan
		and he shall eternal reward
		    all find
			and he shall eternal reward
			    fully obtain,

11	þæs þe he on foldan
	    fremaþ to ryhte.
		so that he on earth
		    acts forth properly.
			because he on earth
			    acts here properly.

Word List

Ænglisc	English
A, a	
and	and
Æ, æ	
æce	eternal
B, b	
belegde	covered
D, d	
dryhten	the-lord
E, e	
ealle	all
eom	am
F, f	
fægere	beautifully
findan	find
foldan	earth
frætewum	ornaments
fremaþ	acts

Ænglisc	English	Ænglisc	English
		R, r	
G, g		ryhte	properly
gefremian	accomplish		
gehwylcre	works	S, s	
gemearcian	to-mark		
gemynde	mindful	sceal	shall
gemyndi	mindful		
gesceop	created	T, t	
geþancie	thank		
		to	to
H, h			
		Þ, þ	
halgungboc	holy-book		
he	he	þæs	so
healde	hold	þam	them
het	ordered	þance	thank
him	him	þe	that
hine	he	þeoda	nations
		þureð	Thureth
I, i		þus	thus
ic	I	W, w	
is	is		
		waldend	ruler
L, l		wurðe	worth
		wyle	wishes
lace	offer	wyrcean	created
lean	reward		
leoht	light		
loue	love		
M, m			
madma	treasures		
mæg	may		
manega	many		
me	me		
metode	the-Creator, the-Creator		
mihta	mighty		
O, o			
on	in, on		

14 The Lord's Prayer I

	Ænglisc	Literal	English

1	...g fæder,
	   þu þe on heofonum eardast,
		...g father,
		   you that in heaven dwell,
			...g father,
			   you that dwell in heaven,

2	geweorðad wuldres dreame.
	
	   Sy þinum weorcum halgad
		make worthy wondrous rejoicing.
		   Be your work hallowed
			make worthy wondrous rejoicing.
			   Be your deeds hallowed

3	noma niþþa bearnum;
	   þu eart nergend wera.
		the name men son;
		   you are saviour of man.
			in the name of men your son;
			   you who are the saviour of man.

4	Cyme þin rice wide,
	   ond þin rædfæst willa
		Come your kingdom wide,
		   and your righteous will
			May your wide kingdom come,
			   and your righteous will

5	aræred under rodores hrofe,
	   eac þon on rumre foldan.
		raise under the heavens a roof,
		   also then in wide earth.
			raise a roof under the heavens,
			   beside the wide earth.

6	Syle us to dæge
	   domfæstne blæd,
		Give us to day
		   judgement-firm glory
			Give us today
			   the glory of your true judgement

7	hlaf userne,
	   helpend wera,
		bread ours,
		   help man,
			our bread,
			   help men,

8	þone singalan,
	   soðfæst meotod.
		those continuously,
		   truth-firm creator.
			those continuously,
			   true creator.

9	Ne læt usic costunga
	   cnyssan to swiðe,
		Do not allow us temptation
		   drive forth exceedingly,
			Do not let us into temptation
			   drive forth exceedingly,

10	ac þu us freodom gief,
	
	   folca waldend,
		nevertheless you us freedom give,
		   folk ruler,
			though you give us freedom,
			
			   ruler of the people,

11	from yfla gehwam,
	   a to widan feore.
		away evil every,
		   eternity to from life.
			away from all evil,
			   from life to eternity.

Word List

Ænglisc	English	Ænglisc	English
A, a			
a	always	cnyssan	drive
ac	nevertheless	costunga	temptation
aræred	raise	cyme	come
		D, d	
B, b			
bearnum	son	dæge	day
blæd	glory	domfæstne	judgement-firm
		dreame	rejoicing
C, c		**E, e**	

Old English Charms, Poems, and Proverbs 1 — The Lord's Prayer I

Ænglisc	English	Ænglisc	English
		on	in
eac	also	ond	and
eardast	dwell		
eart	be	R, r	
F, f		rædfæst	righteous
		rice	kingdom
fæder	father	rodores	the heavens
feore	life	rumre	wide
folca	folk		
foldan	earth	S, s	
freodom	freedom		
from	away	singalan	continuously
		soðfæst	truth-firm
G, g		swiðe	exceedingly
		sy	be
gehwam	every	syle	give
geweorðad	give worthiness to		
gief	give	T, t	
H, h		to	to, forth
halgad	hallowed	Þ, þ	
helpend	help		
heofonum	heaven	þe	that
hlaf	bread	þin	your
hrofe	a roof	þinum	your
		þon	then
L, l		þone	those
		þu	you
læt	allow		
		U, u	
M, m			
		under	under
meotod	creator	us	us
		userne	ours
N, n		usic	us
ne	do not	W, w	
nergend	saviour		
niþþa	men	waldend	ruler
noma	the name	weorcum	work
		wera	of man, man
O, o		widan	wide
		wide	wide

30

Ænglisc	English
willa	will
wuldres	wondrous

Y, y

| *yfla* | evil |

15 Charm 8 For a Swarm of Bees

Ænglisc	Literal	English
1 Wið ymbe nim eorþan, oferweorp mid þinre swiþran	Against a swarm of bees take earth, throw down with your right	Against a swarm of bees take some earth, throwing down with your right
2 handa under þinum swiþran fet, and cwet:	hand under your right foot, and saying:	hand under your right foot, and saying:
3 "Fo ic under fot, funde ic hit.	"Take I under foot, found I it.	"I take this under foot, I found it.
4 Hwæt, eorðe mæg wið ealra wihta gehwilce	Hear, earth may be against all beings every	Hear, earth may be against each and every being
5 and wið andan and wið æminde	and against injury and against forgetfulness	and against injury and against forgetfulness
6 and wið þa micelan".	and against the great".	and against the great".
7 And wiððon forweorp ofer greot, þonne hi swirman, and cweð:	And afterwards throw over earth, those the swarming, and say:	And afterwards throw earth over those swarming and say:
8 "Sitte ge, sigewif, sigað to eorþan!	"Sit you, victorious-women, sink to the earth!	"Sit you, victorious women, sink to the earth!
9 Næfre ge wilde to wuda fleogan.	Never you wild to the woods fly.	Never will you wildly fly to the woods.
10 Beo ge swa gemindige mines godes,	Be you as mindful my wellbeing,	Be as mindful of my wellbeing
11 swa bið manna gehwilc metes and eþeles.	as be men each food and homeland".	as each man is to his food and homeland".

Word List

Ænglisc	English
A, a	
and	and
andan	injury
Æ, æ	
æminde	forgetfulness
B, b	
beo	be
bið	be
C, c	
cweð	say
cwet	saying
E, e	
ealra	all
eorðe	earth
eorþan	earth, the earth
eþeles	homeland
F, f	
fet	foot
fleogan	fly

Old English Charms, Poems, and Proverbs 1   *Charm 8 For a Swarm of Bees*

Ænglisc	English	*Ænglisc*	English
fo	take	*S, s*	
forweorp	throw		
fot	foot	*sigað*	sink
funde	found	*sigewif*	victorious-women
		sitte	sit
G, g		*swa*	as
		swirman	swarming
ge	you	*swiþran*	right
gehwilc	each		
gehwilce	every	*T, t*	
gemindige	mindful		
godes	wellbeing	*to*	to
greot	earth	*tungan*	tongue
H, h		*Þ, þ*	
handa	hand	*þa*	the
hi	the	*þinre*	your
hit	it	*þinum*	your
hwæt	hear	*þonne*	those
I, i		*U, u*	
ic	I	*under*	under
M, m		*W, w*	
mæg	may be	*wið*	against
manna	men	*wiððon*	afterwards
mannes	man's	*wihta*	beings
metes	food	*wilde*	wild
micelan	great	*wuda*	the woods
mid	with		
mines	my	*Y, y*	
N, n		*ymbe*	a swarm of bees
næfre	never		
nim	take		
O, o			
ofer	over		
oferweorp	throw down		

16 Charm 12 Against a Wen

Ænglisc	Literal	English

1 Wenne, wenne,
     wenchichenne,
	Wen, wen,
	     little wen,
		Wen, wen,
		     little wen,

2 her ne scealt þu timbrien,
     ne nenne tun habben,
	here not shall you build,
	     nor any dwelling have,
		you shall not build here,
		     nor have any dwelling,

3 ac þu scealt north eonene
     to þan nihgan berhge,
	but you shall north pass
	     to the next hill,
		but you shall pass north
		     to the next hill,

4 þer þu hauest, ermig,
     enne broþer.
	there you have, in pain,
	     a brother.
		there you have, in pain,
		     a brother.

5 He þe sceal legge
     leaf et heafde.
	He then shall lay
	     a leaf on face.
		He shall then lay
		     a leaf upon your face.

6 Under fot wolues,
     under ueþer earnes,
	Under foot the wolf's,
	     under wing the eagle's,
		Under the wolf's foot,
		     under the eagle's wing,

7 under earnes clea,
     a þu geweornie.
	under eagle's claw,
	     all you wither away.
		under the eagle's claw,
		     and you shall all wither away.

8 Clinge þu
     alswa col on heorþe,
	Shrink you
	     as coal on hearth,
		You will shrink
		     as coal on a hearth,

9 scring þu
     alswa scerne awage,
	shrivel you
	     as dung away,
		you will shrivel
		     as dung away,

10 and weorne
     alswa weter on anbre.
	and evaporate
	     as water in bucket.
		and evapourate
		     as water in a bucket.

11 Swa litel þu gewurþe
     alswa linsetcorn,
	As little you become
	     as linseed,
		You will become as little
		     as linseed,

12 and miccli lesse
     alswa anes handwurmes hupeban,
	and much smaller
	     as a hand-worm's hipbone,
		and much smaller
		     as a hand-worm's hip bone,

13 and alswa litel þu gewurþe
     þet þu nawiht gewurþe.
	and as little you become
	     that you nothing become.
		and become so little
		     that you shall become nothing.

Word List

Ænglisc	English	Ænglisc	English
A, a			
		B, b	
a	all		
ac	but	berhge	hill
alswa	as	broþer	brother
anbre	bucket		
and	and	**C, c**	
anes	a		
awage	away	clea	claw

Ænglisc	English	Ænglisc	English
clinge	shrink	nawiht	nothing
col	coal	ne	not, nor
		nenne	any
E, e		nihgan	next
		north	north
earnes	the eagle's, eagle's		
enne	a	**O, o**	
eonene	pass		
ermig	in pain	on	on, in
et	on		
		S, s	
F, f			
		sceal	shall
fot	foot	scealt	shall
		scerne	dung
G, g		scring	shrivel
		swa	as
geweornie	wither away		
gewurþe	become	**T, t**	
		timbrien	build
H, h		to	to
		tun	dwelling
habben	have		
handwurmes	hand-worm's	**Þ, þ**	
hauest	have		
he	he	þan	the
heafde	face	þe	then
heorþe	hearth	þer	there
her	here	þet	that
hupeban	hipbone	þu	you
L, l		**U, u**	
leaf	a leaf	ueþer	wing
legge	lay	under	under
lesse	smaller		
linsetcorn	linseed	**W, w**	
litel	little		
		wenchichenne	little wen
M, m		wenne	wen
		weorne	evaporate
miccli	much	weter	water
		wolues	the wolf's
N, n			

17 The Partridge

Ænglisc	Literal	English
1 Hyrde ic secgan gen	Heard I told yet	I have yet heard told
bi sumum fugle	about a-certain bird	about a certain bird
2 wundorlicne	wondrous	wondrous
3 fæger,	fair,	fair,
4 þæt word þe gecwæð	that word that said	is the word that was said
wuldres ealdor:	glory lord:	by the Lord of Glory:
5 In swa hwylce tiid	"In so such time	"In such time
swa ge mid treowe to me	as you with faith to me	as you have faith with me
6 on hyge hweorfað,	in soul turn,	and turn with your soul,
ond ge hellfirena	and you hell-fire-like	and you hell-fire
7 sweartra geswicað,	darkness abandon,	and darkness abandon,
swa ic symle to eow	so I forever to you	so I forever to you
8 mid siblufan	with love	with love
sona gecyrre	at once turn	at once will turn
9 þurh milde mod.	by merciful heart.	by merciful heart.
Ge beoð me siþþan	You shall be to me thenceforth	You shall be to me then
10 torhte tireadge	bright glorious	bright glorious
talade ond rimde,	numbered and the host,	numbered with the heavenly host,
11 beorhte gebroþor	bright brethren	bright brethren
on bearna stæl.	in children's place of".	instead of children".
12 Uton we þy geornor	Let us we by this gladly	Let us by this gladly
gode oliccan,	god praise,	praise god,
13 firene feogan,	sin hating,	hating sin,
friþes earnian,	peace earning,	earning peace,
14 duguðe to dryhtne,	virtue to the Lord,	virtue to the Lord,
þenden us dæg scine,	so long as upon us the day shines,	so long as the day shines upon us,
15 þæt swa æþelne	that as nobler	that nobler
eardwica cyst	dwelling place choice	dwelling place we choose
16 in wuldres wlite	in wondrous beauty	in wondrous beauty
wunian motan.	dwelling be allowed to.	to be allowed to dwell.
17 Finit.	The end.	The end.

Word List

Ænglisc	English	Ænglisc	English
Æ, æ		gen	yet
		geornor	gladly
æþelne	nobler	geswicað	abandon
		gode	god
B, b			
		H, h	
bearna	children's		
beoð	shall be	hellfirena	hell-fire-like
beorhte	bright	hweorfað	turn
bi	about	hwylce	such
		hyge	soul
C, c		hyrde	heard
cyst	choice	**I, i**	
D, d		ic	I
		in	in
dæg	the day		
dryhtne	the Lord	**M, m**	
duguðe	virtue		
		me	me, to me
E, e		mid	with
		milde	merciful
ealdor	lord	mod	heart
eardwica	dwelling place	motan	be allowed to
earnian	earning		
eow	you	**O, o**	
F, f		oliccan	praise
		on	in
fæger	fair	ond	and
feogan	hating		
finit	the end	**R, r**	
firene	sin		
friþes	peace	rimde	the host
fugle	bird		
		S, s	
G, g			
		scine	shines
ge	you	secgan	told
gebroþor	brethren	siblufan	love
gecwæð	said	siþþan	thenceforth
gecyrre	turn	sona	at once

Ænglisc	English
stæl	place of
sumum	a-certain
swa	so, as
sweartra	darkness
symle	forever

T, t

talade	numbered
tiid	time
tireadge	glorious
to	to
torhte	bright
treowe	faith

Þ, þ

þæt	that
þe	that
þenden	so long as
þurh	by
þy	by this

U, u

us	upon us
uton	let us

W, w

we	we
wlite	beauty
word	word
wuldres	glory, wondrous
wundorlicne	wondrous
wunian	dwelling

18 Aldhelm

Ænglisc	Literal	English
1 þus me gesette	thus me composed	Thus he composed me
sanctus et iustus	saintly and just	the saintly and just
2 beorn boca gleaw,	nobleman of books learned,	nobleman learned of books,
bonus auctor,	a good author,	a good author,
3 Ealdelm, æþele sceop,	Aldhelm, a noble poet,	Aldhelm, a noble poet,
etiam fuit	also he was	also he was
4 ipselos on æðele	high in nobility	high in nobility
Angolsexna,	of the Anglo-Saxons,	of the Anglo-Saxons,
5 byscop on Bretene.	a bishop in Britain.	a bishop in Britain.
Biblos ic nu sceal,	The book I now shall,	The book I shall now,
6 ponus et pondus	work and weight	a work of weight
pleno cum sensu,	full with sense,	with full sense,
7 geonges geanoðe	youth's meeting	with youth meeting
geomres iamiamque,	mournful right now,	mournfully right now,
8 secgan soð, nalles leas,	tell truly, not at all false,	tell all truly, and not at all falsely,
þæt him symle wæs	that he always to be	that he always had
9 euthenia	prosperity	prosperity
oftor on fylste,	often in support,	often supported
10 æne on eðle	at once in homeland	at once in his homeland
ec ðon ðe se is	though than that he is	even though he is
11 yfel on gesæd.	badly of spoken.	badly spoken of.
Etiam nusquam	Also never	Also never
12 ne sceal ladigan	nor should excuse	nor should excuse
labor quem tenet	work who holds	work who holds
13 encratea,	power-inside,	mastery,
ac he ealneg sceal	but he always shall	but he shall always
14 boethia	Boethius	Boethius
biddan georne	ask eagerly	ask eagerly
15 þurh his modes gemind	for the sake of his mind's thoughts	for the sake of his mind's thoughts
micro in cosmo,	little in the world,	little in the world,
16 þæt him drihten gyfe	that he the Lord gave	that he the Lord gave
dinamis on eorðan,	power on earth,	power on earth
17 fortis factor,	strength maker,	strength maker,
þæt he forð simle	that he forth ever	that he forth forever.

Word List

Ænglisc	English	Ænglisc	English
A, a		eðle	homeland
		encratea	power-inside
ac	but	eorðan	earth
angolsexna	of the Anglo-Saxons	et	and
auctor	author (Latin)	etiam	also (Latin)
		euthenia	prosperity
Æ, æ			
		F, f	
æðele	nobility		
æne	at once	factor	maker (Latin)
æþele	a noble	forð	forth
		fortis	strength (Latin)
B, b		fuit	he was (Latin)
		fylste	support
beorn	nobleman		
biblos	the book (Latin)	**G, g**	
biddan	ask		
boca	of books	geanoðe	meeting
boethia	Boethius	gemind	thoughts
bonus	a good	geomres	mournful
bretene	Britain	geonges	youth's
byscop	a bishop	georne	eagerly
		gesæd	spoken
C, c		gesette	composed
		gleaw	learned
cosmo	the world	gyfe	gave
cum	with (Latin)		
		H, h	
D, d			
		he	he
dinamis	powerful (Latin)	him	he
drihten	the Lord	his	his
Ð, ð		**I, i**	
ðe	that	iamiamque	right now (Latin)
ðon	than	ic	I
		in	in
E, e		ipselos	high (Latin)
		is	is
ealdelm	Aldhelm	iustus	just (Latin)
ealneg	always		
ec	other	**L, l**	

Ænglisc	English	Ænglisc	English
		T, t	
labor	work	tenet	holds (Latin)
ladigan	excuse		
leas	FALSE	Þ, þ	
M, m		þæt	that
me	me	þurh	for the sake of
micro	little (Latin)	þus	thus
modes	mind's		
		W, w	
N, n		wæs	to be
nalles	not at all		
ne	nor	Y, y	
nu	now		
nusquam	never (Latin)	yfel	badly
O, o			
oftor	often		
on	in, of, on		
P, p			
pleno	full (Latin)		
pondus	weight (Latin)		
ponus	work (Latin)		
Q, q			
quem	who (Latin)		
S, s			
sanctus	saintly		
sceal	shall, should		
sceop	poet		
se	he		
secgan	tell		
sensu	sense (Latin)		
simle	ever		
soð	truly		
symle	always		

19 Homiletic Fragment II

	Ænglisc	Literal	English

1	Gefeoh nu on ferðe
	    ond to frofre geþeoh
		Rejoice now in spirit
		    and in satisfaction thrive
			Rejoice now in spirit
			    and thrive in satisfaction

2	dryhtne þinum,
	    ond þinne dom aræl
		the Lord yours,
		    and your glory raise up,
			of your Lord,
			    and raise up in glory,

3	heald hordlocan,
	    hyge fæste bind
		hold hoard-lock,
		    mind fasten bind
			hold the hoard-lock,
			    bind the mind fast

4	mid modsefan.
	    Monig biþ uncuþ
		with spirit.
		    Many be unknowing
			with spirit.
			    Many are unknowing

5	treowgeþofta,
	    teorað hwilum,
		trusted-friends,
		    fail sometimes,
			trusted friends,
			    sometimes they fail,

6	waciaþ wordbeot;
	    swa þeos woruld fareð,
		awaken promise;
		    so this world fares,
			to awaken their word vows,
			    and so fares the world,

7	scurum scyndeð
	    ond gesceap dreogeð.
		storms surged
		    and creation enduring.
			in storms surged
			    and enduring creation.

8	An is geleafa,
	    an lifgende,
		One is faith,
		    one living,
			Faith is one,
			    The living are one,

9	an is fulwiht,
	    an fæder ece,
		one is baptism,
		    one father everlasting,
			The baptism is one,
			    The everlasting father is one,

10	an is folces fruma,
	    se þas foldan gesceop,
		one is the people creator,
		    who this earth made,
			The origin of people is one,
			    who made this earth,

11	duguðe ond dreamas.
	    Dom siþþan weox,
		goods and joys.
		    Judgement afterwards waxed,
			its goods and joys.
			    Judgement waxed afterwards,

12	þeah þeos læne gesceaft
	    longe stode
		though this loaned world
		    for a long time stood
			though this loaned world
			    stood for a long time

13	heolstre gehyded,
	    helme ...edygled,
		dark concealed,
		    shield ...the country,
			concealed in the dark,
			    covered by a shield,

14	biþeaht wel treowum,
	    þystre oferfæðmed,
		surrounded well trees,
		    darkness covered,
			surrounded well by trees,
			    covered with darkness,

15	siþþan geong aweox	afterwards the young grow	afterwards the youth grow

16	mægeð modhwatu
	    mid moncynne;
		maiden strong souled
		    among mankind;
			a maiden strong-souled
			    among mankind

17	ðær gelicade
	    þa... ...op
		there likened
		    then... ...out of
			there likened
			    then… …out of

18	in þam hordfate,
	    halgan gæste,
		in the vessel,
		    holy ghost,
			in the vessel,
			    the holy spirit,

19	beorht on br...
	    ...e scan,
		bright in br...
		    ...e shining,
			bright in …
			    … shining,

20	se wæs ordfruma
	    ealles leohtes.
		he was creator
		    every light.
			he was the creator
			    of all light

Word List

Ænglisc	English	Ænglisc	English
A, a		fulwiht	baptism
an	one	**G, g**	
arær	raise up		
aweox	grow	gæste	ghost
		gefeoh	rejoice
B, b		gehyded	concealed
		geleafa	faith
beorht	bright	gelicade	likened
bind	bind	geong	the young
biþ	be	gesceaft	world
biþeaht	surrounded	gesceap	creation
br	br	gesceop	made
		geþeoh	thrive
D, d			
		H, h	
dom	glory, judgement		
dreamas	joys	halgan	holy
dreogeð	enduring	heald	hold
dryhtne	the Lord	helme	shield
duguðe	goods	heolstre	dark
		hordfate	vessel
Ð, ð		hordlocan	hoard-lock
		hwilum	sometimes
ðær	there	hyge	mind
E, e		**I, i**	
e	e	in	in
ealles	every	is	is
ece	everlasting		
edygled	the country	**L, l**	
		læne	loaned
F, f		leohtes	light
		lifgende	living
fæder	father	longe	for a long time
fæste	fasten		
fareð	fares	**M, m**	
ferðe	spirit		
folces	the people	mægeð	maiden
foldan	earth	mid	among, with
frofre	satisfaction	modhwatu	strong souled
fruma	creator		

Ænglisc	English	Ænglisc	English
modsefan	spirit		
moncynne	mankind	uncuþ	unknowing
monig	many		

N, n

		W, w	
nu	now	waciaþ	awaken
		wæs	was
		wel	well

O, o

		weox	waxed
oferfæðmed	covered	wordbeot	word-vows
on	in	woruld	world
ond	and		
op	out of		
ordfruma	creator		

S, s

scan	shining
scurum	storms
scyndeð	surged
se	he, who
siþþan	afterwards
stode	stood
swa	so

T, t

teorað	fail
to	in
treowgeþofta	trusted-friends
treowum	trees

Þ, þ

þa	then
þam	the
þas	this
þeah	though
þeos	this
þinne	your
þinum	yours
þystre	darkness

U, u

20 Charm 10 For Loss of Cattle

Ænglisc	Literal	English

1 ðis man sceal cweðan ðonne his ceapa hwilcne man for-
2 stolenne. Cwyð ær he ænyg oþer word cweðe:
3 Bethlem hattæ seo burh
    ðe Crist on geboren wes,
4 seo is gemærsod
    ofer ealne middangeard;
5 swa ðeos dæd wyrþe
    for monnum mære,
6 per crucem Christi! And gebide þe ðonne þriwa east and
7 cweð þriwa: Crux Christi ab oriente reducat. And III
8 west and cweð: Crux Christi ab occidente reducat. And
9 III suð and cweð: Crux Christi a meridie reducant. And
10 III norð and cweð: Crux Christi abscondita sunt et inuenta
11 est. Iudeas Crist ahengon, gedidon him dæda þa wyrstan;
12 hælon þæt hi forhelan ne mihton. Swa næfre ðeos dæd
13 forholen ne wyrðe per crucem Christi.
	this a man shall speak when his cattle which man because-stolen. Say before he any other word say:
	Bethlehem is named the town
	    that Christ in born was,
	it is made famous
	    over all middle-earth;
	so this deed worthy
	    for mankind glorious,
	by the cross of Christ! And look it then three-times east and
	say three-times: The cross of Christ from the east led. And three-times
	west and say: The cross of Christ from the west led. And
	three-times south and say: The cross of Christ from the south led. And
	three-times north and say: The cross of Christ was hidden they and found
	is. Judas Christ hung up, did he deeds the worst;
	it that it conceal not might. So never this deed
	hidden not become by the cross of Christ.
		This a man shall speak then for when his cattle is stolen. He shall say this before any other word:
		There is a town called Bethlehem
		    that Christ was born in,
		it is made famous
		    over all of middle-earth;
		so this deed becomes
		    famous for all mankind,
		by the cross of Christ!' And let him look three times to the east and
		say three times: 'The cross of Christ was led from the east'. And three times
		west and say: 'The cross of Christ was led from the west'. And
		three times south and say: 'The cross of Christ was led from the south'. And
		three times north and say: 'The cross of Christ was hidden by them and found it is'. Judas hung up Christ, and he did the worst deeds; that it could not be concealed. So never this deed can become hidden by the cross of Christ

Word List

Ænglisc	English	Ænglisc	English
A, a			
a	from	ænyg	any
ab	from	ær	before
abscondita	was hidden	**B, b**	
ahengon	hung up		
And	and, and	Bethlem	Bethlehem
		burh	town
Æ, æ			

Ænglisc	English	Ænglisc	English
C, c		hælon	hit
ceapa	cattle	hattæ	is named
Christi	of Christ	he	he
Crist	Christ	hi	it
crucem	the cross	him	he
Crux	the cross	his	his
cweð	say	hwilcne	which
cweðan	speak		
cweðe	say	**I, i**	
Cwyð	say		
		III	three-times
D, d		inuenta	found
		is	is
dæd	deed	Iudeas	Judas
dæda	deeds		
		M, m	
Ð, ð			
		mære	famous
ðe	that	man	a man, man
ðeos	this	meridie	the south
ðis	this	middangeard	middle-earth
ðonne	then, when	mihton	might
		monnum	mankind
E, e			
		N, n	
ealne	all		
east	east	næfre	never
est	is	ne	not
et	and	norð	north
F, f		**O, o**	
for	because, for	occidente	the west
forhelan	conceal	ofer	over
forholen	hidden	on	in
		oriente	the east
G, g		oþer	other
gebide	look	**P, p**	
geboren	born		
gedidon	did	per	by
gemærsod	made famous		
		R, r	
H, h			

Ænglisc	English
reducant	led
reducat	led

S, s

sceal	shall
seo	it, the
stolenne	stolen
suð	south
sunt	they
swa	so

Þ, þ

þa	the
þæt	that
þe	it
þriwa	three-times

W, w

wes	was
west	west
word	word
wyrðe	become
wyrstan	worst
wyrþe	become

21 Charm 7 For the Water-Elf Disease

Ænglisc	Literal	English
1 *Gif mon biþ on wæterælfadle, þonne beoþ him þa hand-*	If one be in water elf disease, whereby be his being hand-	If one has water elf disease, where his hand
2 *næglas wonne and þa eagan tearige and wile locian niþer.*	nails dark and being eyes teary and willing to look downwards.	nails are dark and his eyes are teary and willing to look downwards.
3 *Do him þis to læcedome: eoforþrote, cassuc, fone nioþo-*	Do him this to remedy: carline thistle, cassock, take from below-	Do him this remedy: carline thistle, cassock, take from below
4 *weard, eowberge, elehtre, eolone, merscmealwan crop,*	keep, yew berry, lupine, elecampane, marshmallow sprout,	keep, yew berry, lupine, elecampane, marshmallow sprout,
5 *fenminte, dile, lilie, attorlaþe, polleie, marubie, docce, ellen,*	fen mint, dill, lily, cock's spur grass, pennyroyal, marrabulum, sorrel, elder,	fen mint, dill, lily, cock's spur grass, pennyroyal, marrabulum, sorrel, elder,
6 *felterre, wermod, streawbergean leaf, consolde; ofgeot mid*	felterry, wormwood, strawberry leaf, comfrey; soak with	felterry, wormwood, strawberry leaf, comfrey; soak with
7 *ealaþ, do hæligwæter to, sing þis gealdor ofer þriwa:*	ale, do holy water to, sing this chant over three times:	ale, add holy water to, and sing this chant over it three times:
8 *Ic benne awrat betest beadowræda,*	I this wound wrote the best battle bandage,	I have written for this wound the best battle bandage,
9 *swa benne ne burnon, ne burston,*	so the wound does not burn, nor burst,	so the wound does not burn, nor burst,
10 *ne fundian, ne feologan,*	neither forwards, nor become fallow,	neither forwards, nor becoming fallow,
11 *ne hoppettan, ne wund waxsian,*	neither throb, nor wound geow,	neither throb, nor wound grow,
12 *ne dolh diopian; ac him self healde halewæge,*	nor the pain deepen; but he himself hold the hallows,	nor the pain deepen; but he himself holds the hallows,
13 *ne ace þe þon ma, þe eorþan on eare ace.*	nor grow though from there greater, though the earth in ears grows.	nor grow though from there any greater, though the earth in ears grows.
14 *Sing þis manegum siþum: Eorþe þe onbere eallum hire*	Sing this many afterwards: Earth though withers all these	Sing this many times afterwards: 'Though the earth withers, all these
15 *mihtum and mægenum. þas galdor mon mæg singan on*	might and power. this chant one may sing over	might and power'. This chant one may sing over
16 *wunde.*	wounds.	the wounds.

Word List

Ænglisc	English
A, a	
ac	but
ace	grow, grows
and	and
attorlaþe	cock's spur grass
awrat	wrote
B, b	
beadowræda	battle bandage
benne	the wound, this wound
beoþ	be
betest	the best
biþ	be
burnon	burn
burston	burst
C, c	
cassuc	cassock
consolde	comfrey
crop	sprout
D, d	
dile	dill
diopian	deepen
do	do
docce	sorrel
dolh	the pain
E, e	
eagan	eyes
ealaþ	ale
eallum	all
eare	ears
elehtre	lupine
ellen	elder
eoforþrote	carline thistle
eolone	elecampane
eorþan	the earth
eorþe	earth
eowberge	yew berry
F, f	
felterre	felterry
fenminte	fen mint
feologan	become fallow
fone	take
fundian	forwards
G, g	
galdor	chant
gealdor	chant
gif	if
H, h	
hæligwæter	holy water
halewæge	the hallows
hand	hand
healde	hold
him	he, him, his
hire	these
hoppettan	throb
I, i	
ic	I
L, l	
læcedome	remedy
leaf	leaf
lilie	lily
locian	to look
M, m	

Ænglisc	English	Ænglisc	English
ma	greater	þas	this
mæg	may	þe	though
mægenum	power	þis	this
manegum	many	þon	from there
marubie	marrabulum	þonne	whereby
merscmealwan	marshmallow	þriwa	three times
mid	with		
mihtum	might	**W, w**	
mon	one		
		wæteræelfadle	water elf disease
N, n		waxsian	grow
		weard	keep
næglas	nails	wermod	wormwood
ne	does not, neither, nor	wile	willing
nioþo	from below	wonne	dark
niþer	downwards	wund	wound
		wunde	wounds

O, o

ofer	over
ofgeot	soak
on	in, over
onbere	withers

P, p

polleie	pennyroyal

S, s

self	himself
sing	sing
singan	sing
siþum	afterwards
streawbergean	strawberry
swa	so

T, t

tearige	teary
to	to

Þ, þ

þa	being

22 Wulf and Eadwacer

	Ænglisc	Literal	English
1	Leodum is minum / swylce him mon lac gife;	The people that are mine / such is he one offered a gift;	To my people / as if someone gave them a gift;
2	willað hy hine aþecgan, / gif he on þreat cymeð.	will they him to kill, / if he in a troop arrives.	they want to kill him, / if he arrives in a troop.
3	Ungelic is us.	Unlike it is to us.	It is different for us.
4	Wulf is on iege, / ic on oþerre.	Wulf is on island, / I on another.	Wulf is on an island, / and I am on another.
5	Fæst is þæt eglond, / fenne biworpen.	Fastened is that island, / by fens surrounded.	Secured is that island, / surrounded by fens.
6	Sindon wælreowe / weras þær on ige;	They are bloodthirsty / men there on the island;	They are bloodthirsty / the men there on the island;
7	willað hy hine aþecgan, / gif he on þreat cymeð.	will they him to kill, / if he in a troop arrives.	they want to kill him, / if he arrives in a troop.
8	Ungelice is us.	Unlike it is to us.	It is different for us.
9	Wulfes ic mines widlastum / wenum dogode;	To Wulf I mine far-wandering / hopes for days;	To my Wulf I with far-wandering / hopes for days;
10	þonne hit wæs renig weder / ond ic reotugu sæt,	whenever it was rainy weather / and I mournfully sat,	whenever it was rainy weather / and I sat mournfully,
11	þonne mec se beaducafa / bogum bilegde,	whenever I the brave-warrior's / arms covered,	whenever the brave warrior's / arms covered me,
12	wæs me wyn to þon, / wæs me hwæþre eac lað.	was to me delight to that, / was to me however also loathsome.	that was a delight to me, / but was also painful.
13	Wulf, min Wulf, / wena me þine	Wulf, my Wulf, / hopes mine to you	Wulf, my Wulf, / my hopes for you
14	seoce gedydon, / þine seldcymas,	a sickness did, / your seldom-coming,	have caused a sickness, / your infrequent visits,
15	murnende mod, / nales meteliste.	mournful mood, / never food-lacking.	a mournful spirit, / never lacking in food.
16	Gehyrest þu, Eadwacer? / Uncerne earne hwelp	Hear you, Eadwacer? / Ours somewhere a cub	Do you hear, Eadwacer? / Somewhere our cub
17	bireð Wulf to wuda.	bears Wulf to the woods.	is carried by a wolf to the woods
18	þæt mon eaþe tosliteð / þætte næfre gesomnad wæs,	that one easily tears-apart / that never together was,	that is easily torn apart / by that which was never together,
19	uncer giedd geador.	our poem together.	our poem together.

Word List

Ænglisc	English	Ænglisc	English
A, a		H, h	
aþecgan	to kill	he	he
		him	is he
B, b		hine	him
		hit	it
beaducafa	brave-warrior's	hwæþre	however
bilegde	covered	hwelp	a cub
bireð	bears	hy	they
biworpen	surrounded		
bogum	arms	I, i	
C, c		ic	I
		iege	island
cymeð	arrives	ige	the island
		is	is, it is, that are
D, d		L, l	
dogode	for days	lac	offered
		laþ	loathsome
E, e		leodum	the people
eac	also		
eadwacer	Eadwacer (a name)	M, m	
earne	somewhere		
eaþe	easily	me	mine, to me
eglond	island	mec	I
		meteliste	food-lacking
F, f		min	my
		mines	mine
fæst	fastened	minum	mine
fenne	by fens	mod	mood
		mon	one
G, g		murnende	mournful
geador	together	N, n	
gedydon	did		
gehyrest	hear	næfre	never
gesomnad	together	nales	never
giedd	poem		
gif	if	O, o	
gife	a gift		
		on	in, on

Ænglisc	English	Ænglisc	English
ond	and	weder	weather
oþerre	another	wena	hopes
		wenum	hopes
R, r		weras	men
		widlastum	far-wandering
renig	rainy	willað	will
reotugu	mournfully	wuda	the woods
		wulf	Wulf (a name)
S, s		wulfes	to Wulf (a name)
		wyn	delight
sæt	sat		
se	the		
seldcymas	seldom-coming		
seoce	a sickness		
sindon	they are		
swylce	such		

T, t

| to | to |
| toslited | tears-apart |

Þ, þ

þær	there
þæt	that
þætte	that
þine	to you, your
þon	that
þonne	whenever
þreat	a troop
þu	you

U, u

uncer	our
uncerne	ours
ungelic	unlike
ungelice	unlike
us	to us

W, w

| wælreowe | bloodthirsty |
| wæs | was |

23 The Coronation of Edgar

	Ænglisc	Literal	English

1	Her Eadgar wæs,
	    Engla waldend,
		Here Edgar was,
		    English ruler,
			Here Edgar was,
			    ruler of the English,

2	corðre miclum
	    to cyninge gehalgod
		assembly great
		    to king consecrated
			in a great assembly
			    consecrated as king

3	on ðære ealdan byrig,
	    Acemannesceastre;
		in there old town,
		    Akeman's Town;
			in the old down,
			    Akeman's Town;

4	eac hi igbuend
	    oðre worde
		also the islanders
		    another word
			also the islanders
			    by another word

5	beornas Baðan nemnaþ.
	    þær wæs blis micel
		children-of-men Bath name.
		    there was rejoicing much
			children of men call it Bath.
			    there was much rejoicing

6	on þam eadgan dæge
	    eallum geworden,
		about that blessed day
		    all became,
			about that blessed day
			    come to all,

7	þone niða bearn
	    nemnað and cigað
		the conflict children
		    name and call
			those children of conflict
			    name and call it

8	Pentecostenes dæg.
	    þær wæs preosta heap,
		Pentecost day.
		    there was priests pile,
			Pentecost day.
			    there was a throng of priests

9	micel muneca ðreat,
	    mine gefrege,
		great monk crowd,
		    of mind noted,
			a great crowd of monks
			    of learned minds,

10	gleawra gegaderod.
	    And ða agangen wæs
		skilful gathered.
		    And then going was
			and skilful gathered
			    And then had gone

11	tyn hund wintra
	    geteled rimes
		ten hundred winters
		    reckoned counted
			ten hundred winters
			    reckoned to be counted

12	fram gebyrdtide
	    bremes cyninges,
		from the-birth
		    celebrated king,
			from the birth
			    of the celebrated king,

13	leohta hyrdes,
	    buton ðær to lafe þa get
		light keeper,
		    except there to remain then agreed
			keeper of lights,
			    except there remained it was agreed

14	wæs wintergeteles,
	    þæs ðe gewritu secgað,
		was winters-numbered,
		    this as writings say,
			there were winters numbered,
			    as the writings say

15	seofon and twentig;
	    swa neah wæs sigora frean
		seven and twenty;
		    so nigh was victories lord
			twenty seven;
			    So nigh on had the Lord of Victories

16	ðusend aurnen,
	    ða þa ðis gelamp.
		thousand passed,
		    then that this happened.
			a thousand years passed,
			    when this happened.

17	And him Eadmundes
	    eafora hæfde
		And he Edmund
		    descendants had
			And his Edmund's
			    descendants had

18	nigon and XX,
	    niðweorca heard,
		nine and twenty,
		    conflict bitter,
			twenty nine,
			    in bitter conflict,

19	wintra on worulde,
	    ða þis geworden wæs,
		winters in the-world,
		    then it agreed was,
			winters in the world,
			    then it was agreed,

20	and þa on ðam XXX wæs
	    ðeoden gehalgod.
		and then in that thirty was
		    the-lord consecrated.
			that then in that thirty years
			    the Lord was consecrated.

Word List

Ænglisc	English
A, a	
acemannesceastre	Akeman's Town
agangen	going
and	and
aurnen	passed
B, b	
baðan	Bath
bearn	children
beornas	children-of-men
blis	rejoicing
bremes	celebrated
buton	except
byrig	town
C, c	
cigað	call
corðre	assembly
cyninge	king
cyninges	king
D, d	
dæg	day
dæge	day
Ð, ð	
ða	then
ðær	there
ðære	there
ðam	that
ðe	as
ðis	this
ðreat	crowd
ðusend	thousand
E, e	
eac	also

Ænglisc	English
eadgan	blessed
eadgar	Edgar
eadmundes	Edmund's
eafora	descendants
ealdan	old
eallum	all
engla	English
F, f	
fram	from
frean	lord
G, g	
gebyrdtide	the-birth
gefrege	noted
gegaderod	gathered
gehalgod	consecrated
gelamp	happened
get	agreed
geteled	reckoned
geworden	agreed, became
gewritu	writings
gleawra	skilful
H, h	
hæfde	had
heap	pile
heard	bitter
her	here
hi	the
him	his
hund	hundred
hyrdes	keeper
I, i	
igbuend	islanders
L, l	

Ænglisc	English	Ænglisc	English
lafe	remain		
leohta	light	Þ, þ	
M, m		þa	that, then
		þær	there
micel	great, much	þæs	this
miclum	great	þam	that
mine	of mind	þeoden	the-lord
muneca	monk	þis	it
		þone	the
N, n			
		W, w	
neah	nigh		
nemnað	name	wæs	was
nemnaþ	name	waldend	ruler
niða	murmuring	wintergeteles	winters-numbered
niðweorca	conflict	wintra	winters
nigon	nine	worde	word
		worulde	the-world
O, o			
		X, x	
oðre	another		
on	about, in	xx	twenty
		xxx	thirty
P, p			
pentecostenes	Pentecost		
preosta	priests		
R, r			
rimes	counted		
S, s			
secgað	say		
seofon	seven		
sigora	victories		
swa	so		
T, t			
to	to		
twentig	twenty		
tyn	ten		

24 Durham

	Ænglisc	Literal	English
1	Is ðeos burch breome geond Breotenrice,	Is this city famous over Britain-kingdom,	This city is famous over the Kingdom of Britain,
2	steppa gestaðolad, stanas ymbutan	steps founded, stones about	with steps founded with stones about
3	wundrum gewæxen. Weor ymbeornad,	wondrously grown. The Wear beholds,	wondrously grown. The Wear beholds,
4	ea yðum stronge, and ðer inne wunað	river waves strong, and there in dwell	a river of strong waves, and therein dwell
5	feola fisca kyn on floda gemonge.	many fish kinds in flood together.	many kinds of fish in the floods together.
6	And ðær gewexen is wudafæstern micel;	And there grown is wood-fastened great;	And there is grown great forests;
7	wuniad in ðem wycum wilda deor monige,	live in they dwellings wild beasts many,	There living in the dwellings many wild beasts,
8	in deope dalum deora ungerim.	in deep dales deer innumerable.	in deep dales inumerable deer.
9	Is in ðere byri eac bearnum gecyðed	Is in this city also children well-known	Also in this city well known to children of men
10	ðe arfesta eadig Cudberch	the merciful blessed Cuthbert	the merciful blessed Cuthbert
11	and ðes clene cyninges heafud,	and this clean king's head,	and this chaste king's head,
12	Osuualdes, Engle leo, and Aidan biscop,	Oswald's, Angli lion, and Aidan bishop,	Oswald, the lion of the Angli, and Biship Aidan,
13	Eadberch and Eadfrið, æðcle geferes.	Eadbert and Eadfrid, noble associates.	Eadbert and Eadfrid, the noble associates.
14	Is ðer inne midd heom æðelwold biscop	Is there in the middle with them Aethelwold bishop	There in among them Bishop Aethelwold
15	and breoma bocera Beda, and Boisil abbot,	and celebrated writer of books Bede, and Boisil abbot,	and celebrated writer of books Bede, and Abbot Boisil,
16	ðe clene Cudberte on gecheðe	as clean Cuthbert in youth	as chaste Cuthbert in youth
17	lerde lustum, and he his lara wel genom.	learned joyfully, and he his learning well took.	learned joyfully, and he took his learning well.
18	Eardiæð æt ðem eadige in in ðem minstre	Inhabited at these blessed in the-chamber these ministers	Inhabited these blessed chamber these ministers
19	unarimeda reliquia,	unnumbered relics,	unnumbered relics,
20	ðær monia wundrum gewurðað,	that many wondrous being,	that many being wondrous,

	Ænglisc	Literal	English
21	ðes ðe writ seggeð, midd ðene drihnes wer domes bideð.	these that writings say, with the Lord's man judgement awaits.	so the writings say, with the Lord's people judgement awaits.

Word List

Ænglisc	English	Ænglisc	English
A, a		deope	deep
		deor	beasts
abbot	abbot	deora	deer
aidan	Aidan	domes	judgement
and	and	drihnes	Lord's
arfesta	merciful		
		Ð, ð	
Æ, æ			
		ðær	that, there
æðele	noble	ðe	as, that, the
æðelwold	Aethelwold	ðem	these, they
æt	at	ðene	the
		ðeos	this
B, b		ðer	there
		ðere	this
bearnum	children	ðes	these, this
beda	Bede		
bideð	awaits	E, e	
biscop	bishop		
bocera	writer of books	ea	river
boisil	Boisil	eac	also
breoma	celebrated	eadberch	Eadbert
breome	famous	eadfrið	Eadfrid
breotenrice	Britain-kingdom	eadig	blessed
burch	city	eadige	blessed
byri	city	eardiæð	inhabited
		engle	Angli
C, c			
		F, f	
clene	clean		
cudberch	Cuthbert	feola	many
cudberte	Cuthbert	fisca	fish
cyninges	king's	floda	flood
D, d		G, g	
dalum	dales	gecheðe	youth

Ænglisc	English	Ænglisc	English
gecyðed	well-known	osuualdes	Oswald's
geferes	associates		
gemonge	together	**R, r**	
genom	took		
geond	over	reliquia	relics
gestaðolad	founded		
gewæxen	grown	**S, s**	
gewexen	grown		
gewurðað	being	seggeð	say
		stanas	stones
H, h		steppa	steps
		stronge	strong
he	he		
heafud	head	**U, u**	
heom	with them		
his	his	unarimeda	unnumbered
		ungerim	innumerable
I, i			
		W, w	
in	in, the-chamber		
inne	in	wel	well
is	is	weor	the Wear
		wer	man
K, k		wilda	wild
		writ	writings
kyn	kinds	wudafæstern	wood-fastened
		wunað	dwell
L, l		wundrum	wondrous, wondrously
lara	learning	wuniad	live
leo	lion	wycum	dwellings
lerde	learned		
lustum	joyfully	**Y, y**	
M, m		yðum	waves
		ymbeornad	beholds
micel	great	ymbutan	about
midd	the middle, with		
minstre	ministers		
monia	many		
monige	many		
O, o			
on	in		

25 Charm 5 For Loss of Cattle

Ænglisc	Literal	English
1 þonne þe mon ærest secge þæt þin ceap sy losod, þonne	then that someone first says that your property is lost, then	When someone first says that your property is lost, then
2 cweð þu ærest, ær þu elles hwæt cweþe:	say you first, before you anything-else hear say:	you say first, before you say anything else:
3 Bæðleem hatte seo buruh þe Crist on acænned wæs,	Bethlehem named the town that Christ in brought-forth was,	The town is called Bethlehem where Christ was born,
4 seo is gemærsod geond ealne middangeard;	it is made-famous around all middle-earth;	and it is famous around all the earth;
5 swa þyos dæd for monnum mære gewurþe	so this deed before men distinguished become	so this deed for mankind became distinguished
6 þurh þa haligan Cristes rode! Amen. Gebide þe þonne	through the holy Christ's cross! Amen. Abide then from-there	through the holy Christ's cross! Amen. Look then from there
7 þriwa east and cweþ þonne þriwa: Crux Christi ab oriente	three-times east and say then three-times: The cross of Christ from the east	three times east and then say three times: The cross of Christ from the east
8 reducað. Gebide þe þonne þriwa west and cweð þonne	is led. Abide then there three-times west and say there	is led. Look then there three times west and say there
9 þriwa: Crux Christi ab occidente reducat. Gebide þe	three-times: The cross of Christ from the west is led. Abide then	three times: The cross of Christ from the west is led. Look then
10 þonne þriwa suð and cweþ þriwa: Crux Christi ab austro	from there three-times south and say three-times: The cross of Christ from the south	from there three times south and say three times: The cross of Christ from the south
11 reducat. Gebide þonne þriwa norð and cweð þriwa: Crux	is led. Abide then three-times north and say three-times: The cross	is led. Look then three times north and say three times: The cross
12 Christi ab aquilone reducað, crux Christi abscondita est et	of Christ from the north is led, the cross of Christ hidden is and	of Christ from the north is led, the cross of Christ is hidden and
13 inuenta est. Iudeas Crist ahengon, dydon dæda þa	found is. Judas Christ hung up, doing deeds the	is found. Judas hung up Christ, doing the deeds
14 wyrrestan, hælon þæt hy forhelan ne mihtan. Swa þeos	worst, covering that he hidden not might. So this	the worst, covering so that he could not be hidden. So this
15 dæd nænige þinga forholen ne wurþe þurh þa haligan	deed none thing hidden not become through the holy	deed nothing may become hidden through the holy
16 Cristes rode. Amen.	Christ's cross. Amen.	Christ's cross. Amen.

Word List

Ænglisc	English
A, a	
ab	from (Latin)
abscondita	hidden (Latin)
acænned	brought-forth
ahengon	hung up
amen	amen
and	and
aquilone	the north (Latin)
austro	the south (Latin)
Æ, æ	
ær	before
ærest	first
B, b	
bæðleem	Bethlehem
buruh	town
C, c	
ceap	property
christi	of Christ
crist	Christ
cristes	Christ's
crux	the cross (Latin)
cweð	say
cweþ	say
cweþe	say
D, d	
dæd	deed
dæda	deeds
dydon	doing
E, e	
ealne	all
east	east
elles	anything-else

Ænglisc	English
est	is (Latin)
et	and (Latin)
F, f	
for	for
forhelan	hidden
forholen	hidden
G, g	
gebide	abide
gemærsod	made-famous
geond	around
gewurþe	become
H, h	
hælon	covering
haligan	holy
hatte	named
hwæt	hear
hy	he
I, i	
inuenta	found (Latin)
is	is
iudeas	Judas
L, l	
losod	lost
M, m	
mære	distinguished
middangeard	middle-earth
mihtan	might
mon	someone
monnum	mankind
N, n	

Ænglisc	English
nænige	none
ne	not
norð	north

O, o

occidente	the west (Latin)
on	in
oriente	the east (Latin)

R, r

reducað	is led (Latin)
reducat	is led (Latin)
rode	cross

S, s

secge	says
seo	it, the
suð	south
swa	so
sy	is

Þ, þ

þa	the
þæt	that
þe	that, then
þeos	this
þin	your
þinga	thing
þonne	from there, from-there, then, there
þriwa	three-times
þu	you
þurh	through
þyos	this

W, w

wæs	was
west	west
wurþe	become
wyrrestan	worst

26 Charm 9 For Loss of Cattle

	Ænglisc	Literal	English
1	Ne forstolen ne forholen nanuht, þæs ðe ic age, þe ma ðe	Not stolen not hidden nothing, of-that which I own, any more which	May nothing be stolen or hidden which I own, any more than
2	mihte Herod urne drihten. Ic geþohte sancte Eadelenan	might Herod our Lord. I thought Saint Blessed-Helen	Herod might our Lord. I thought of the blessed Saint Helen
3	and ic geþohte Crist on rode ahangen; swa ic þence þis feoh	and I thought Christ on cross hanged; thus I think this cattle	and I thought of Christ hanged on the cross; thus I think to this cattle
4	to findanne, næs to oðfeorrganne, and to witanne, næs to	to find, by-no-means to drive-away, and to protect, by-no-means to	to find, not to drive away, and to protect, not to
5	oðwyrceanne, and to lufianne, næs to oðlædanne.	destroy, and to love, by-no-means to lead-off.	destroy, to love, not to lead away.
6	Garmund, godes ðegen,	Garmund, God's thane,	Garmund, God's servant,
7	find þæt feoh and fere þæt feoh	find that cattle and drive that cattle	find that cattle and drive that cattle
8	and hafa þæt feoh and heald þæt feoh	and have that cattle and hold that cattle	and have that cattle and hold that cattle
9	and fere ham þæt feoh.	and drive home that cattle.	and drive home that cattle.
10	þæt he næfre næbbe landes, þæt he hit oðlæde,	that he never not-have land, that he it lead-off,	so that he may not have land, that he may lead it away,
11	ne foldan, þæt hit oðferie,	not earth, that he drive-off,	nor earth, that he may drive it away,
12	ne husa, þæt he hit oðhealde.	not houses, that he it keep-away.	nor any houses, that he may keep it away.
13	Gif hyt hwa gedo, ne gedige hit him næfre!	If it who do, not prosper it him never!	If anyone would do this, may they never prosper from it!
14	Binnan þrym nihtum cunne ic his mihta,	Within three nights know I his might,	Within three nights I will know his powers,
15	his mægen and his mihta and his mundcræftas.	his strengths and his powers and his protection-powers.	his strengths and his powers and his powers of protection.
16	Eall he weornige, swa syre wudu weornie,	All he waste-away, as rotten wood waste-away,	May he all waste away, as rotten wood waste away,
17	swa breðel seo swa þystel,	as brittle be as thistle,	be as brittle as a thistle,
18	se ðe ðis feoh oðfergean þence	he who this cattle drive-away intend	he who this cattle might intend to drive away
19	oððe ðis orf oðehtian ðence.	or this cattle disposess intent.	or this cattle might have intent to disposess.
20	Amen.	Amen.	Amen.

Word List

Ænglisc	English	Ænglisc	English
A, a			
age	own	**G, g**	
ahangen	hanged	garmund	Garmund (a name)
amen	amen	gedige	prosper
and	and	gedo	do
		geþohte	thought
B, b		gif	if
		godes	God's
binnan	within		
breðel	brittle	**H, h**	
		hafa	have
C, c		ham	home
crist	Christ (a name)	he	he
cunne	know	heald	hold
		herod	Herod (a name)
D, d		him	him
		his	his
drihten	lord	hit	he, it
		husa	houses
Ð, ð		hwa	who
		hyt	it
ðe	which, who		
ðegen	thane	**I, i**	
ðence	intent		
ðis	this	ic	I
E, e		**L, l**	
eadelenan	Blessed-Helen (a name)	landes	land
eall	all	lufianne	love
F, f		**M, m**	
		ma	more
feoh	cattle	mægen	strengths
fere	drive	mihta	might, powers
find	find	mihte	might
findanne	find	mundcræftas	protection-powers
foldan	earth		
forholen	hidden	**N, n**	
forstolen	stolen		

Ænglisc	English	Ænglisc	English
næbbe	not-have	þystel	thistle
næfre	never		
næs	by-no-means	U, u	
nanuht	nothing		
ne	not	urne	our
nihtum	nights		
		W, w	
O, o			
		weornie	waste-away
oððe	or	weornige	waste-away
oðehtian	disposess	witanne	protect
oðfeorrganne	drive-away	wudu	wood
oðfergean	drive-away		
oðferie	drive-off		
oðhealde	keep-away		
oðlædanne	lead-off		
oðlæde	lead-off		
oðwyrceanne	destroy		
on	on		
orf	cattle		
R, r			
rode	cross		
S, s			
sancte	saint		
se	he		
seo	be		
swa	as, thus		
syre	rotten		
T, t			
to	to		
Þ, þ			
þæs	of-that		
þæt	that		
þe	any		
þence	intend, think		
þis	this		
þrym	three		

27 Charm 3 Against a Dwarf

	Ænglisc	Literal	English
1	Wið dweorh man sceal niman VII lytle oflætan, swylce	Against a dwarf one shall take seven little wafers, such as	Against a dwarf one must take seven little wafers, such as
2	man mid ofrað, and writan þas naman on ælcre oflætan:	one with offertory, and write these names on each wafer:	the one makes offertory with, and write these names on each wafer:
3	Maximianus, Malchus, Iohannes, Martimianus, Dionisius	Maximianus, Malchus, Iohannes, Martimianus, Dionisius	Maximianus, Malchus, Iohannes, Martimianus, Dionisius,
4	Constantinus, Serafion. þænne eft þæt galdor, þæt	Constantinus, Serafion. Then after that chant, that	Constantinus, Serafion. Then after that chant, that
5	her æfter cweð, man sceal singan, ærest on þæt wynstre	here after say, one shall sing, first in the left	which is here after said, one shall sing, first in the left
6	eare, þænne on þæt swiðre eare, þænne bufan þæs mannes	ear, then in the right ear, then above the person's	ear, then in the right ear, then above the person's
7	moldan. And ga þænne an mædenman to and ho hit on	top-of-the-head. And let then a maiden go to and hang it about	top of the head. And then let a maiden go to them and hang it about
8	his sweoran, and do man swa þry dagas; him bið sona sel.	his neck, and do one so three days; to-him be soon better.	his neck, and do so for three days, he will soon be better.

9	Her com in gangan,
	    inswiden wiht,
		Here came in walking,
		    singed creature,
			Here came in walking,
			    a singed creature,

10	hæfde him his haman on handa,
	    cwæð þæt þu his hæncgest wære,
		had he his horse-collar in hand,
		    saying that you his horse were,
			he had his horse collar in hand,
			    saying that you were his horse,

11	legde þe his teage an sweoran.
	    Ongunnan him of þæm lande liþan;
		laid then his ties on neck.
		    Began he of that land journey;
			he then laid his ties on your neck.
			    He began a land journey;

12	sona swa hy of þæm lande coman,
	    þa ongunnan him ða liþu colian.
		as soon as they of that land came,
		    then began he the limbs became-cold.
			as soon as they came from the land,
			    then the limbs began to cool.

13	þa com in gangan
	    dweores sweostar;
		Then came in walking
		    the dwarf's sister;
			Then came walking in
			    the dwarf's sister;

14	þa geændade heo
	    and aðas swor
		then interceded she
		    and oaths swore
			then she interceded
			    and swore oaths

15	ðæt næfre þis ðæm adlegan
	    derian ne moste,
		that never this the sick-person
		    harm not be able to,
			that this beast may never the sick person
			    be able to harm,

16	ne þæm þe þis galdor
	    begytan mihte,
		nor they that this chant
		    obtain might,
			nor the one who this chant
			    might obtain,

17	oððe þe þis galdor
	    ongalan cuþe.
		or that this chant
		    recite be able to.
			or that this chant
			    is able to recite.

18	Amen. Fiað.	Amen. Let it be so.	Amen. Let it be so.

Word List

Ænglisc	English	Ænglisc	English
A, a		ðæt	that
aðas	oaths	**E, e**	
adlegan	sick-person		
amen	amen	eare	ear
an	a, on	eft	after
and	and		
		F, f	
Æ, æ			
		fiað	let it be so
æfter	after		
ælcre	each	**G, g**	
ærest	first		
		ga	let
B, b		galdor	chant
		gangan	walking
begytan	obtain	geændade	interceded
bið	be		
bufan	above	**H, h**	
C, c		hæfde	had
		hæncgest	horse
colian	became-cold	haman	horse-collar
com	came	handa	hand
coman	came	heo	she
constantinus	Constantinus	her	here
cuþe	be able to	him	he, to-him
cwæð	saying	his	his
cweð	say	hit	it
		ho	hang
D, d		hy	they
dagas	days	**I, i**	
derian	harm		
dionisius	Dionisius	in	in
do	do	inswiden	singed
dweores	the dwarf's	iohannes	Iohannes
dweorh	a dwarf		
		L, l	
Đ, ð			
		lande	land
ða	the	legde	laid
ðæm	the	liþan	journey

Ænglisc	English	Ænglisc	English
liþu	limbs	swylce	such as
lytle	little		
M, m		**T, t**	
mædenman	maiden	teage	ties
malchus	Malchus	to	go to
man	one		
mannes	person's	**Þ, þ**	
martimianus	Martimianus		
maximianus	Maximianus	þa	then
mid	with	þæm	that, they
mihte	might	þænne	then
moldan	top-of-the-head	þæs	the
moste	be able to	þæt	that, the
		þas	these
N, n		þe	that, then
		þis	this
næfre	never	þry	three
naman	names	þu	you
ne	nor, not		
niman	take	**V, v**	
O, o		vii	seven
oððe	or	**W, w**	
of	of		
oflætan	wafer, wafers	wære	were
ofrað	offertory	wið	against
on	about, in, on	wiht	creature
ongalan	recite	writan	write
ongunnan	began	wynstre	left
S, s			
sceal	shall		
sel	better		
serafion	Serafion		
singan	sing		
sona	as soon, soon		
swa	as, so		
sweoran	neck		
sweostar	sister		
swiðre	right		
swor	swore		

28 A Summons to Prayer

	Ænglisc	Literal	English

1	þænne gemiltsað þe, N.,
	    mundum qui regit,
		then have mercy you, (name),
		    the world who rules,
			Then he will have mercy upon you, (name),
			    who rules the world,

2	ðeoda þrymcyningc
	    thronum sedentem
		nations the ruling king
		    the throne sitting on
			the ruling king of nations
			    sitting on the throne

3	a butan ende	a without end	without end
4	saule þinre	soul yours	your soul

5	Geunne þe on life
	    auctor pacis
		Grant you in life
		    author of peace
			May he grant you in life
			    the author of peace

6	sibbe gesælða,
	    salus mundi,
		joys of peace,
		    salvation of the world,
			the joys of peace,
			    the salvation of the world,

7	metod se mæra
	    magna uirtute,
		creator the famous
		    great virtue,
			the famous creator
			    of great virtue,

8	and se soðfæsta
	    summi filius
		and the truth-fastened
		    highest son
			and righteous
			    the highest son

9	fo on fultum,
	    factor cosmi,
		receive in comfort,
		    maker of the world,
			receive (you) in comfort,
			    the maker of the world,

10	se of æþelre wæs
	    uirginis partu
		who of noble was
		    maiden birth
			who was of noble
			    maiden birth

11	clæne acenned
	    Christus in orbem,
		clean born
		    Christ into the world,
			born chaste
			    Christ to the world,

12	metod þurh Marian,
	    mundi redemptor,
		creator through Mary,
		    the world's redeemer,
			the creator through Mary,
			    the world's redeemer,

13	and þurh þæne halgan gast.
	    Uoca frequenter
		and through the holy spirit.
		    Call frequently
			and through the holy spirit.
			    Call frequently

14	bide helpes hine,
	    clemens deus,
		pray for help him,
		    clement God,
			pray to him for help,
			    clement God,

15	se onsended wæs
	    summo de throno
		who sent was
		    highest of thrones
			who was sent
			    from the highest of thrones

16	and þære clænan
	    clara uoce
		and to the clean
		    clear voice
			and to the chaste
			    clear voice

17	þa gebyrd bodade
	    bona uoluntate
		the birth heralded
		    good will
			the birth heralded
			    of good will

18	þæt heo scolde cennan
	    Christum regem,
		that she should bear
		    Christ the king,
			that she should bear
			    Christ the king,

19	ealra cyninga cyningc,
	    casta uiuendo.
		all kings king of,
		    chaste living.
			the king of all kings,
			    of chaste living.

20	and þu þa soðfæstan
	    supplex rogo,
		And you as truth-fastened
		    supplicant pray,
			And you as righteous
			    supplicant pray,

21	fultumes bidde friclo
	    uirginem almum,
		eagerly ask aid
		    the virgin nurturing,
			ask eagerly for aid
			    from the nurturing virgin,

22	and þær æfter to
	    omnes sancti
		and there after to
		    all the saints
			and there after to
			    all the saints

	Ænglisc	Literal	English
23	bliðmod bidde, beatus et iustus,	blithe-minded pray, blessed and just,	gentle-minded pray, blessed and just,
24	þæt hi ealle þe unica uoce	that they all for you one voice	that they all for you with one voice
25	þingian to þeodne thronum regentem,	intercede to the prince the throne ruling,	intercede to the prince ruling the throne,
26	æcum drihtne, alta polorum,	eternal lord, heights of the poles,	eternal lord, the heights of the heavens,
27	þæt he þine saule, summus iudex,	that he your soul, highest judge,	that he your soul, the highest judge,
28	onfo freolice, factor aeternus,	receive freely, maker eternal,	receive freely, the eternal creator,
29	and he gelæde luce perhennem,	and he leads light perpetual,	and he leads into eternal light,
30	þær eadige animæ sanctæ	there blessed souls holy	there where blessed holy souls
31	rice restað regna caelorum.	kingdom rest kingdom of heaven.	rest in the kingdom, the kingdom of heaven.

Word List

Ænglisc	English	Ænglisc	English
A, a		bliðmod	blithe-minded
		bodade	heralded
a	a	bona	good (Latin)
acenned	born	butan	without
aeternus	eternal (Latin)		
almum	nurturing (Latin)	**C, c**	
alta	heights		
and	and	caelorum	of heaven (Latin)
animæ	souls (Latin)	casta	chaste
auctor	author (Latin)	cennan	bear
		christum	Christ (Latin)
Æ, æ		christus	Christ (Latin)
		clænan	clean
æcum	eternal	clæne	clean
æfter	after	clara	clear (Latin)
æþelre	noble	clemens	clement (Latin)
		cosmi	of the world (Latin)
B, b		cyninga	kings
		cyningc	king of
beatus	blessed (Latin)		
bidde	ask, pray	**D, d**	
bide	pray		

Old English Charms, Poems, and Proverbs 1 *A Summons to Prayer*

Ænglisc	English	*Ænglisc*	English
de	of (Latin)	I, i	
deus	god (Latin)		
drihtne	lord	in	into
		iudex	judge (Latin)
Ð, ð		iustus	just (Latin)
ðeoda	nations	L, l	
E, e		life	life
		luce	light (Latin)
eadige	blessed		
ealle	all	M, m	
ealra	all		
ende	end	mæra	famous
et	and (Latin)	magna	great (Latin)
		marian	Mary
F, f		metod	creator
		mundi	of the world (Latin), the world's (Latin)
factor	maker (Latin)		
filius	son (Latin)	mundum	the world (Latin)
fo	receive		
freolice	freely	N, n	
frequenter	frequently (Latin)		
friclo	aid	n	(name)
fultum	comfort		
fultumes	eagerly	O, o	
G, g		of	of
		omnes	all (Latin)
gast	spirit	on	in
gebyrd	birth	onfo	receive
gelæde	leads	onsended	sent
gemiltsað	have mercy	orbem	the world (Latin)
gesælða	of peace		
geunne	grant	P, p	
H, h		pacis	of peace (Latin)
		partu	birth
halgan	holy	perhennem	perpetual
he	he	polorum	of the poles (Latin)
helpes	for help		
heo	she	Q, q	
hi	they		
hine	him	qui	who (Latin)
		R, r	

Ænglisc	English	Ænglisc	English
		þinre	yours
redemptor	redeemer (Latin)	þrymcyningc	the ruling king
regem	the king (Latin)	þu	you
regentem	ruling (Latin)	þurh	through
regit	rules (Latin)		
regna	kingdom (Latin)	**U, u**	
restað	rest		
rice	kingdom	uirginem	the virgin (Latin)
rogo	pray (Latin)	uirginis	maiden (Latin)
		uirtute	virtue (Latin)
S, s		uiuendo	living (Latin)
		unica	one (Latin)
salus	salvation (Latin)	uoca	call (Latin)
sanctæ	holy (Latin)	uoce	voice (Latin)
sancti	the saints (Latin)	uoluntate	will (Latin)
saule	soul		
scolde	should	**W, w**	
se	the, who		
sedentem	sitting on (Latin)	wæs	was
sibbe	joys		
soðfæsta	truth-fastened		
soðfæstan	truth-fastened		
summi	highest (Latin)		
summo	highest (Latin)		
summus	highest (Latin)		
supplex	supplicant (Latin)		

T, t

throno	thrones
thronum	the throne, the throne
to	to

Þ, þ

þa	as, the
þæne	the
þænne	then
þær	there
þære	to the
þæt	that
þe	for you, you
þeodne	the prince
þine	your
þingian	intercede

29 The Death of Edward

	Ænglisc	Literal	English
1	*Her Eadward kingc, Engla hlaford,*	Here Edward the king, English lord,	Here Edward the king, lord of the English
2	*sende soþfæste sawle to Criste*	sent righteous soul to Christ	sent his righteous soul to Christ
3	*on godes wæra, gast haligne.*	in God's keeping, spirit holy.	in God's keeping, and the holy spirit.
4	*He on worulda her wunode þrage*	He in the world here dwelt for a time	He in the world here dwelt for a time
5	*on kyneþrymme, cræftig ræda,*	in royal-power, skilful counsel,	in royal power, with skilful counsel,
6	*XXIIII, freolic wealdend,*	twenty four, freely ruling,	twenty four, freely ruling,
7	*wintra gerimes, weolan britnode,*	winters number, wealth bestowed,	winters numbered, bestowed wealth,
8	*and healfe tid, hæleða wealdend,*	and half a time, saviour ruler,	and half a time saviour ruling,
9	*weold wel geþungen Walum and Scottum*	ruling well gracefully the Welsh and the Scots	ruled well and gracefully the Welsh and the Scots
10	*and Bryttum eac, byre æðelredes,*	and the Britons too, his child Æthelred's,	and the Britons too, his child Æthelred's,
11	*Englum and Sexum, oretmægcum,*	The Angles and The Saxons, warriors,	the Angles and the Saxons, warriors,
12	*swa ymbclyppað cealde brymmas,*	as embraced cold waves,	as embraced cold waves
13	*þæt eall Eadwarde, æðelum kinge,*	that all Edward, noble king,	that all Edward, noble king,
14	*hyrdon holdlice hagestealde menn.*	obeyed graciously young and brave men.	graciously obeyed young and brave men.
15	*Wæs a bliðemod bealuleas kyng,*	Was ever blithe-mood the innocent king,	Was ever in joyful mood the innocent king,
16	*þeah he lange ær, lande bereafod,*	though he long before, of land bereft,	though he long before, bereft of land,
17	*wunode wræclastum wide geond eorðan,*	dwelt outcast widely over the earth,	dwelt as an outcast widely over the earth,
18	*syððan Cnut ofercom kynn æðelredes*	since Canute overcame kin Æthelred's	since Canute overcame Æthelred's kin
19	*and Dena weoldon deore rice*	and Danes ruled the dear kingdom	and the Danes ruled the dear kingdom
20	*Engla landes XXVIII*	Engla Land twenty-eight	England twenty eight
21	*wintra gerimes, welan brytnodon.*	winters numbered, wealth bestowed.	winters numbered, wealth bestowed.
22	*Syððan forð becom*	Since forth came	Since forth came

The Death of Edward

	Ænglisc	Literal	English
	freolice in geatwum	splendid in trappings	splendid in trappings
23	kyningc kystum god,	a king of virtues good,	a king of virtues good,
	clæne and milde,	chaste and mild,	chaste and mild,
24	Eadward se æðela,	Edward the noble,	Edward the noble,
	eðel bewerode,	country defended,	defended the country,
25	land and leode,	land and people,	land and people,
	oðþæt lungre becom	until suddenly came	until suddenly came
26	deað se bitera,	death so bitter,	a death so bitter,
	and swa deore genam	and so dear seized	and so dear seized
27	æþelne of eorðan;	noble of the earth;	noble of the earth;
	englas feredon	angels carried	angels carried
28	soþfæste sawle	righteous soul	his righteous soul
	innan swegles leoht.	into heaven's light.	into heaven's light.
29	And se froda swa þeah	And the wise as nevertheless	and the wise nevertheless
	befæste þæt rice	entrusted the kingdom	entrusted the kingdom
30	heahþungenum menn,	high-ranking man,	a high-ranking man,
	Harolde sylfum,	Harold himself,	Harold himself,
31	æþelum eorle,	noble earl,	the noble earl,
	se in ealle tid	who in all time	who in all time
32	hyrde holdlice	obeyed loyally	obeyed loyally
	hærran sinum	lord his	his lord's
33	wordum and dædum,	words and deeds,	words and deeds,
	wihte ne agælde	anything not delaying	not delaying in anything
34	þæs þe þearf wæs	that the necessary was	that was necessary to
	þæs þeodkyninges.	this great-king.	this great king.

Word List

Ænglisc	English	Ænglisc	English
A, a		**B, b**	
a	ever	bealuleas	the innocent
agælde	delaying	becom	came
and	and	befæste	entrusted
		bereafod	bereft
Æ, æ		bewerode	defended
		bitera	bitter
æðela	noble	bliðemod	blithe-mood
æðelredes	Æthelred's	britnode	bestowed
æðelum	noble	brymmas	waves
ær	before	brytnodon	bestowed
æþelne	noble	bryttum	the Britons
æþelum	noble	byre	his child

Ænglisc	English	Ænglisc	English
C, c		god	good
		godes	God's
cealde	cold		
clæne	chaste	**H, h**	
cnut	Canute		
cræftig	skilful	hæleða	saviour
criste	Christ	hærran	lord
		hagestealde	young and brave
D, d		haligne	holy
		harolde	Harold
dædum	deeds	he	he
deað	death	heahþungenum	high-ranking
dena	the Danes	healfe	half
deore	dear, the dear	her	here
		hlaford	lord
E, e		holdlice	graciously, loyally
		hyrde	obeyed
eac	too	hyrdon	obeyed
eadward	Edward		
eadwarde	Edward	**I, i**	
eall	all		
ealle	all	in	in
eðel	country	innan	into
engla	Engla, english		
englas	angels	**K, k**	
englum	the Angles		
eorðan	the earth	kingc	the king
eorle	earl	kinge	king
		kyneþrymme	royal-power
F, f		kyng	king
		kyningc	a king
feredon	carried	kynn	kin
forð	forth	kystum	of virtues
freolic	freely		
freolice	splendid	**L, l**	
froda	wise		
		land	land
G, g		lande	of land
		landes	Land
gast	spirit	lange	long
geatwum	trappings	leode	people
genam	seized	leoht	light
geond	over	lungre	suddenly
gerimes	number, numbered		
geþungen	gracefully	**M, m**	

Ænglisc	English	Ænglisc	English
		þeah	nevertheless, though
menn	man, men	þearf	necessary
milde	mild	þeodkyninges	great-king
		þrage	for a time
N, n			
		W, w	
ne	not		
		wæra	keeping
O, o		wæs	was
		walum	the Welsh
oðþæt	until	wealdend	ruler
of	of	wel	well
ofercom	overcame	welan	wealth
on	in	weolan	wealth
oretmægcum	warriors	weold	ruling
		weoldon	ruled
R, r		wide	widely
		wihte	anything
ræda	counsel	wintra	winters
rice	kingdom	wordum	words
		worulda	the world
S, s		wræclastum	outcast
		wunode	dwelt
sawle	soul		
scottum	the Scots	**X, x**	
se	so, the, who		
sende	sent	xxiiii	twenty four
sexum	the Saxons	xxviii	twenty-eight
sinum	his		
soþfæste	righteous	**Y, y**	
swa	as, so		
swegles	heaven's	ymbclyppað	embraced
syððan	since		
sylfum	himself		
T, t			
tid	a time, time		
to	to		
Þ, þ			
þæs	that, this		
þæt	that, the		
þe	the		

30 Waldere B

	Ænglisc	Literal	English
1	"mece bæteran	"Sword better	"a better sword
2	buton ðam anum ðe ic eac hafa	except the one which I also have	except the one which I also have
3	on stanfate stille gehided.	in jewelled-sheath quietly hidden.	in a jewelled sheath quietly hidden.
4	Ic wat þæt hit ðohte ðeodric Widian	I know that of it thought Theodric to Widia	I know that of it thought Theodric to Widia
5	selfum onsendon, and eac sinc micel	himself to send, and also riches many	himself to send, and also many riches
6	maðma mid ði mece, monig oðres mid him	treasure with the sword, many other with it	treasure with the sword, many others with it
7	golde gegirwan (iulean genam),	gold adorned (reward taken),	gold adorned (the reward was taken),
8	þæs ðe hine of nearwum Niðhades mæg,	because of him from captivity Nithad's kinsman,	because of him from captivity Nithhad's kinsman,
9	Welandes bearn, Widia ut forlet;	Weland's son, Widia out released;	Weland's son, Widia released (him);
10	ðurh fifela geweald forð onette".	through a monster's domain forth hasten".	through the domain of a monster hasten forth".
11	Waldere maðelode, wiga ellenrof,	Waldere spoke, warrior courageous,	Waldere spoke, the courageous warrior,
12	hæfde him on handa hildefrofre,	had he in hands weapon,	he had in his hands the battle-comfort (weapon),
13	guðbilla gripe, gyddode wordum:	battle-bill gripped, spoke words:	battle-bill (blade) in his grip, he spoke the words:
14	Hwæt! ðu huru wendest, wine Burgenda,	"Indeed! you surely expected, friend Of the Burgundians,	"Indeed! you surely expected, friend of the Burgundians,
15	þæt me Hagenan hand hilde gefremede	that me Hagen's hand battle prevail	that against me Hagen's hand would prevail in battle
16	and getwæmde feðewigges.	and separate foot-battle.	and separate me from the fray.
	Feta, gyf ðu dyrre,	Take, if you dare,	Take, if you dare,
17	æt ðus heaðuwerigan hare byrnan.	from me thus battle-weary grey armour.	from me thus battle-weary the grey armour.
18	Standeð me her on eaxelum ælfheres laf,	Stands on me here about shoulders Ælfhere's legacy,	It stands here on my shoulders Ælfhere's legacy,
19	god and geapneb, golde geweorðod,	good and cleverly-woven, gold adorned,	good and cleverly woven, adorned with gold
20	ealles unscende æðelinges reaf	all blameless noble's vestment	a wholly blameless prince's vestment

	Ænglisc	Literal	English
21	to habbanne, þonne hand wereð	to have, when hand protects	to have, when his hand protects
22	feorhhord feondum.	his soul-hoard his enemies.	his soul-hoard from his enemies.
	Ne bið fah wið me,	Not be hostile against me,	It will not be hostile to me,
23	þonne me unmægas eft ongynnað,	when to me unrelated again assail,	when men unrelated again assail,
24	mecum gemetað, swa ge me dydon.	sword meet with, as you me did.	meet me with swords, as you did to me.
25	ðeah mæg sige syllan se ðe symle byð	yet may victory give he who always be	Yet he may give victory, he who is ever
26	recon and rædfest ryhta gehwilces.	ready and sound rights matters	ready and sound in council in every matter of right
27	Se ðe him to ðam halgan helpe gelifeð,	He that the to the holy one help trusts,	He who to that holy one trusts for help,
28	to gode gioce, he þær gearo findeð	to God's support, he there ready finds	to God for support, he finds it ready there
29	gif ða earnunga ær geðenceð.	if that earning first considers.	if he has earnt it first he considers.
30	þonne moten wlance welan britnian,	then may the proud wealth dispense,	They may the proud dispense wealth,
31	æhtum wealdan, þæt is..."	possessions rule over, that is..."	rule over possessions, that is..."

Word List

Ænglisc	English	Ænglisc	English
A, a		bið	be
		britnian	dispense
and	and	burgenda	of the Burgundians
anum	one	buton	except
		byð	be
Æ, æ		byrnan.	armour
æðelinges	noble's	**D, d**	
æhtum	possessions		
ælfheres	Ælfhere's	dydon.	did
ær	first	dyrre	dare
æt	from me		
		Ð, ð	
B, b			
		ða	that
bæteran	better	ðam	the
bearn	son	ðe	of, that, which, who

Ænglisc	English	Ænglisc	English
ðeah	yet	gif	if
ðeodric	Theodric	gioce	support
ði	the	god	good
ðohte	thought	God's	God's
ðu	you	golde	gold
ðurh	through	gripe	gripped
ðus	thus	guðbilla	battle-bill
		gyddode	spoke
E, e		gyf	if
eac	also	**H, h**	
ealles	all		
earnunga	earning	habbanne	have
eaxelum	shoulders	hæfde	had
eft	again	hafa	have
ellenrof	courageous	hagenan	Hagen's
		halgan	holy one
F, f		hand	hand
		handa	hands
fah	hostile	hare	grey
feðewigges	foot-battle	he	he
feondum.	his enemies	heaðuwerigan	battle-weary
feorhhord	soul-hoard	helpe	help
feta	take	her	here
fifela	a monster's	hilde	battle
findeð	finds	hildefrofre	weapon
forð	forth	him	he, it, the
forlet;	released	hine	him
		hit	of it
G, g		huru	surely
		hwæt	indeed
ge	you		
geapneb	cleverly-woven	**I, i**	
gearo	ready		
geðenceð.	considers	ic	I
gefremede	prevail	is	is
gegirwan	adorned	iulean	reward
gehided.	hidden		
gehwilces	matters	**L, l**	
gelifeð	trusts		
gemetað	meet with	laf	legacy
genam	taken		
getwæmde	separate	**M, m**	
geweald	domain		
geweorðod	adorned	maðelode	spoke

Ænglisc	English	Ænglisc	English
maðma	treasure	T, t	
mæg	kinsman, may		
me	me, on me, to me	to	to
mece	Sword		
mecum	sword	Þ, þ	
micel	many		
mid	with	þær	there
monig	many	þæs	because
moten	may	þæt	that
		þonne	then, when
N, n			
		U, u	
ne	not		
nearwum	captivity	unmægas	unrelated
niðhades	Nithad's	unscende	blameless
		ut	out
O, o			
		W, w	
oðres	other		
of	from	waldere	Waldere
on	about, in	wat	know
onette	hasten	wealdan	rule over
ongynnað	assail	welan	wealth
onsendon	to send	welandes	Weland's
		wendest	expected
R, r		wereð	protects
		wið	against
rædfest	sound	widia	Widia
reaf	vestment	widian	to Widia
recon	ready	wiga	warrior
rhyta	rights	wine	friend
		wlance	the proud
S, s		wordum	words
se	he		
selfum	himself		
sige	victory		
sinc	riches		
standeð	stands		
stanfate	jewelled-sheath		
stille	quietly		
swa	as		
syllan	give		
symle	always		

31 Waldere A

	Ænglisc	Literal	English
1	*hyrde hyne georne:*	Encouraged him eagerly:	(she) encouraged him eagerly:
2	*"Huru Welande...*	"Truly Weland's...	"Truly Weland's
	worc ne geswiceð	work will-not fail	work will not fail
3	*monna ænigum*	Man any	Any man
	ðara ðe Mimming can	those who Mimming can	of those who can Mimming
4	*heardne gehealdan.*	Hard-warrior hold.	The hard warrior hold.
	Oft æt hilde gedreas	Often in battle fell	Often in battle fell
5	*swatfag and sweordwund*	Blood-stained and sword-wounded	Blood-stained and sword wounded
	secg æfter oðrum.	warrior after another.	one warrior after another.
6	*ætlan ordwyga,*	Intended warrior,	Intended warrior,
	ne læt ðin ellen nu gy...	not let your courage now yet...	now do not let your courage
7	*gedreosan to dæge,*	Perish to day,	Perish today,
	dryhtscipe	valour	valour
8	*is se dæg cumen*	Is the day coming	Now the day has come
9	*þæt ðu scealt aninga*	That you shall must-do	When you must do
	oðer twega,	of two-things,	one of two things,
10	*lif forleosan*	Life for-lose	Lose your life
	oððe l\<an\>gne dom	or long glory	or long lasting glory
11	*agan mid eldum,*	Achieve with men,	Achieve among the men,
	ælfheres sunu.	Aelfhere's (name) son.	Aelfhere's son.
12	*Nalles ic ðe, wine min,*	Not-at-all I you, friend mine,	Not at all would I you, my friend,
	wordum cide,	words chide,	chide with words,
13	*ðy ic ðe gesawe*	That I you saw	That I saw you
	æt ðam sweordplegan	at that sword-play	at sword-play
14	*ðurh edwitscype*	In disgrace	In disgrace
	æniges monnes	any man's	from any man's
15	*wig forbugan*	Battle for-surrendering	Battle surrender
	oððe on weal fleon,	or on the-wall fleeing,	or fleeing to the ramparts
16	*lice beorgan,*	Body defend,	To defend your body,
	ðeah þe laðra fela	though however foes many	though many foes
17	*ðinne byrnhomon*	Your armour	At your armour
	billum heowun,	sword hew,	hewed with swords
18	*ac ðu symle furðor*	But you always further	But you always further
	feohtan sohtest,	fighting sought,	sought the fighting,
19	*mæl ofer mearce;*	Measure over limit;	Measure over the limit;
	ðy ic ðe metod ondred,	therefore I to-you the-creator dreaded,	therefore for you I feared the creator,
20	*þæt ðu to fyrenlice*	That you too savagely	That you too savagely
	feohtan sohtest	fighting sought	sought the fighting

Ænglisc	Literal	English

21 æt ðam ætstealle
    oðres monnes,
	At the waypoint
	    another man's,
		At the waypoint
		    with another man,

22 wigrædenne.
    Weorða ðe selfne
	Warfare.
	    Worthiness to yourself
		Warfare.
		    Bring honour to yourself

23 godum dædum,
    ðenden ðin god recce.
	Good deeds,
	    as-long-as you god cares-for.
		With good deeds,
		    as long as god cares for you.

24 Ne murn ðu for ði mece;
    ðe weard maðma cyst
	Not fear you for your sword;
	    that worthy treasure choice
		Do not be fearful for your sword;
		    that worthy choice of treasures

25 gifeðe to geoce,
    mid ðy ðu Guðhere scealt
	Given to support,
	    with it you Guthere's shall
		Given as support,
		    with it you shall Guthere's

26 beot forbigan,
    ðæs ðe he ðas beaduwe ongan
	Boast humiliate,
	    this which he this battle undertook
		Boast humiliate,
		    since he undertook this strife

27 \<mi\>d unryhte
    ærest secan.
	With un-right
	    first to-seek.
		With wrong
		    first to seek.

28 Forsoc he ðam swurde
    and ðam syncfatum,
	Refused he that sword
	    and that precious-treasures,
		He refused the sword
		    and the precious treasures,

29 beaga mænigo,
    nu sceal bega leas
	Rings many,
	    now shall ring less
		Many rings,
		    now he shall ringless

30 hworfan from ðisse hilde,
    hlafurd secan
	Turn from this battle,
	    lord seek
		Turn from this battle,
		    the lord must seek

31 ealdne éðel
    oððe her ær swefan,
	Old homeland
	    or here before death-sleep,
		His old homeland
		    or sleep before here in death,

32 gif he ða..."	If he then..."	If he then..."

Word List

Ænglisc	English	Ænglisc	English
A, a		ænigum	any
		ær	before
ac	but	ærest	first
agan	achieve	æt	at, in
and	and	ætlan	intended
aninga	must-do	ætstealle	waypoint
Æ, æ		B, b	
æfter	after	beaduwe	battle
ælfheres	Aelfhere's (name)	beaga	rings
æniges	any	bega	ring

Ænglisc	English	Ænglisc	English
beorgan	defend		
beot	boast	F, f	
billum	sword		
byrnhomon	armour	fela	many
		feohtan	fighting
C, c		fleon	fleeing
		for	for
can	can	forbigan	humiliate
cide	chide	forbugan	for-surrendering
cumen	coming	forleosan	for-lose
cyst	choice	forsoc	refused
		from	from
D, d		furðor	further
		fyrenlice	savagely
dædum	deeds		
dæg	day	G, g	
dæge	day		
dom	glory	gedreas	fell
dryhtscipe	valour	gedreosan	perish
		gehealdan	hold
Ð, ð		geoce	support
		georne	eagerly
ða	then	gesawe	saw
ðæs	this	geswiceð	fail
ðam	that, the	gif	if
ðara	those	gifeðe	given
ðas	this	god	god
ðe	that, to, to-you, which, who, you	godum	good
		Guðhere	Guthcrc's (name)
ðeah	though	gy	yet
ðenden	as-long-as		
ði	your	H, h	
ðin	you, your		
ðinne	your	he	he
ðisse	this	heardne	hard-warrior
ðu	you	heowun	hew
ðurh	in	her	here
ðy	it, that, therefore	hilde	battle
		hlafurd	lord
E, e		huru	truly
		hworfan	turn
ealdne	old	hyne	him
edwitscype	disgrace	hyrde	encouraged
eldum	men		
ellen	courage	I, i	
ethel	homeland		

Ænglisc	English	Ænglisc	English
		ordwyga	warrior
ic	I		
is	is	**R, r**	
L, l		recce	cares-for
		S, s	
langne	long		
laðra	foes	sceal	shall
læt	let	scealt	shall
leas	less	se	the
lice	body	secan	seek, to-seek
lif	life	secg	warrior
		selfne	yourself
M, m		sohtest	sought
		sunu	son
mid	with	swatfag	blood-stained
maðma	treasure	swefan	death-sleep
mæl	measure	sweordplegan	sword-play
mænigo	many	sweordwund	sword-wounded
mearce	limit	swurde	sword
mece	sword	symle	always
metod	the-creator	syncfatum	precious-treasures
Mimming	Mimming (name)		
min	mine	**T, t**	
monna	man		
monnes	man's	to	to, too
murn	fear	twega	two-things
N, n		**Þ, þ**	
nalles	not-at-all		
ne	not, will-not	þæt	that
nu	now	þe	however
O, o		**U, u**	
oððe	or	unryhte	un-right
oðer	of		
oðres	another	**W, w**	
oðrum	another		
ofer	over	weal	the-wall
oft	often	wearð	worthy
on	on	Welande	Weland's (name)
ondred	dreaded	weorða	worthiness
ongan	undertook	wig	battle

Ænglisc	English
wigrædenne	warfare
wine	friend
worc	work
wordum	words

32 The Death of Alfred

Ænglisc	Literal	English
Her com Ælfred, se unsceððiga æþeling, Æþelrædes sunu cinges, hider inn and wolde to his meder, þe on Wincestre sæt, ac hit him ne geþafode Godwine eorl, ne ec oþre men þe mycel mihton wealdan, forðan hit hleoðrode þa swiðe toward Haraldes, þeh hit unriht wære.	Here came Alfred, so innocent prince, Aethelred's son the-king's, here in and wished to his mother, who in Winchester settled, but this he was-not permitted Godwin earl, nor also the-other men as much might wielded, because he spoke then very-much toward Harald, though it un-right was.	Here came Alfred, innocent prince, son of King Aethelred, came into the country and wished to see his mother who lived in Winchester, but this was not permitted by Earl Godwin, nor the other men (barons) welding much might had spoke very much toward Harald, thought this was wrong.

1. *Ac Godwine hine þa gelette and hine on hæft sette,*
   So Godwin he then hindered and he in captivity set,
   So Godwin then hindered and set him in captivity,

2. *and his geferan he todraf, and sume mislice ofsloh;*
   And his companions he destroyed, and some-of various-ways slayed;
   And he destroyed his companions, and slayed them in various ways;

3. *sume hi man wið feo sealde, sume hreowlice acwealde,*
   Some-of the men against livestock sold, some-of cruelly killed,
   Some of the men were sold for livestock, some of them were cruelly killed,

4. *sume hi man bende, sume hi man blende,*
   Some-of the men bound, some-of the men blinded,
   Some of them were bound, some of them were blinded,

5. *sume hamelode, sume hættode.*
   Some mutilated, some scalped.
   Some mutilated, some scalped,

6. *Ne wearð dreorlicre dæd gedon on þison earde,*
   Not became bloodier deed done in this land,
   There was no bloodier deed, done in this land,

7. *syþþan Dene comon and her frið namon.*
   Since The-Danes came and here peace took.
   Since the Danes came and took peace here.

8. *Nu is to gelyfenne to ðan leofan gode,*
   Now is to believe to the love God,
   Now it is to be believed to the love of God,

9. *þæt hi blission bliðe mid Criste*
   That the bliss joyous with Christ
   That the bliss of joy with Christ

10. *þe wæron butan scylde swa earmlice acwealde.*
    Though were without fault so miserably killed.
    Though were without fault so miserably killed.

11. *Se æþeling lyfode þa gyt; ælc yfel man him gehet,*
    The prince lived yet still; every evil man he had,
    The prince lived yet still; and he had the evil of every man,

12. *oðþæt man gerædde þæt man hine lædde*
    Until man advisement that man they led
    Until under a man's advisement they led that man

13. *to Eligbyrig swa gebundenne.*
    To Ely-in-the-Fens as bound.
    To Ely-in-the-Fens so bound.

Ænglisc	Literal	English
14 *Sona swa he lende,*	Soon as he landed,	As soon as he landed,
on scype man hine blende,	on ship man him blinded,	on a ship a man blinded him,
15 *and hine swa blindne*	And he so blinded	And so he was blinded
brohte to ðam munecon,	brought to the monks,	brought to the monks,
16 *and he þar wunode*	And he there dwelled	And he dwelled there
ða hwile þe he lyfode.	then while then he lived.	as long as he lived.
17 *Syððan hine man byrigde,*	Afterwards he men buried,	Afterwards men buried him,
swa him wel gebyrede,	so his well birth,	befitting his noble birth,
18 *ful wurðlice,*	Full worthiness,	With full worthiness,
swa he wyrðe wæs,	as he worthy was,	as he was worthy,
19 *æt þam westende,*	At the west-end,	At the west end,
þam styple ful gehende,	then steeple full close-by,	of the steeple, close by,
20 *on þam suðportice;*	About the south-porch;	About the south porch;
seo saul is mid Criste.	his soul is with Christ.	his soul is with Christ.

Word List

Ænglisc	English	Ænglisc	English
A, a		**C, c**	
ac	but, so	*cinges*	the-king's
acwealde	killed	*com*	came
and	and	*comon*	came
		Criste	Christ (name)
Æ, æ			
ælc	every	**D, d**	
Ælfred	Alfred (name)	*dæd*	deed
æt	at	*Dene*	the-Danes
æþeling	prince	*dreorlicre*	bloodier
Æþelrædes	Aethelred's (name)		
		Ð, ð	
B, b		*ða*	then
		ðam	the
bende	bound	*ðan*	the
blende	blinded		
bliðe	joyous	**E, e**	
blindne	blinded		
blission	bliss	*earde*	land
brohte	brought	*earmlice*	miserably
butan	without	*ec*	also
byrigde	buried		

Ænglisc	English	Ænglisc	English
Eligbyrig	Ely-in-the-Fens (place)	inn	in
eorl	earl	is	is

F, f

L, l

Ænglisc	English	Ænglisc	English
feo	livestock	lædde	led
forðan	because	lende	landed
frið	peace	leofan	love
ful	full	lyfode	lived

G, g

M, m

Ænglisc	English	Ænglisc	English
gebundenne	bound	man	man, men
gebyrede	birth	meder	mother
gedon	done	men	men
geferan	companions	mid	with
gehende	close-by	mihton	might
gehet	had	mislice	various-ways
gelette	hindered	munecon	monks
gelyfenne	believe	mycel	much
gerædde	advisement		
geþafode	permitted		

N, n

Ænglisc	English
gode	God (name)
Godwine	Godwin (name)
gyt	still

Ænglisc	English
namon	took
ne	nor, not, was-not
nu	now

H, h

O, o

Ænglisc	English	Ænglisc	English
hæft	captivity	oðþæt	until
hættode	scalped	ofsloh	slayed
hamelode	mutilated	on	about, in, on
Haraldes	Harald (name)	oþre	the-other
he	he		
her	here		
hi	the		

S, s

Ænglisc	English
hider	here
him	he, his
hine	he, him, they
his	his
hit	he, it, this
hleoðrode	spoke
hreowlice	cruelly
hwile	while

Ænglisc	English
sæt	settled
saul	soul
scylde	fault
scype	ship
se	so, the
sealde	sold
seo	his
sette	set

I, i

Ænglisc	English	Ænglisc	English
Sona	soon	wyrðe	worthy
styple	steeple		
suðportice	south-porch	Y, y	
sume	some, some-of		
sunu	son	yfel	evil
swa	as, so		
swiðe	very-much		
Syððan	afterwards		
syþþan	since		

T, t

to	to
todraf	destroyed
toward	toward

Þ, þ

þa	then, yet
þæt	that
þam	the, the, then
þar	there
þe	as, then, though, who
þeh	though
þison	this

U, u

unriht	un-right
unsceððiga	innocent

W, w

wære	was
wæron	were
wæs	was
wealdan	wielded
wearð	became
wel	well
westende	west-end
wið	against
Wincestre	Winchester (place)
wolde	wished
wunode	dwelled
wurðlice	worthiness

Word List (Ænglisc to English)

Ænglisc	English

A, a

Ænglisc	English
a	a, all, always, ever, from
ab	from, from (Latin)
abbot	abbot
abolescit	fades-away (Latin)
abscondita	hidden (Latin), was hidden
ac	but, nevertheless, so
acænned	brought-forth
ace	grow, grows
acemannesceastre	Akeman's Town
acenned	born
acolað	grows-cold
acwealde	killed
aðas	oaths
Aðelwold	Æthelwold (a name)
adlegan	sick-person
adwæsce	quenched
aðystrað	grows-dark
aeðða	or
aefter	after, after
aelda	elders'
aer	before, before, first
aerist	first
aeternus	eternal (Latin)
afera	heir-of
agælde	delaying
agan	achieve
agangen	going
age	own
ahangen	hanged
ahengon	hung up
aidan	Aidan
alaðaþ	becomes-loathed
allmectig	almighty
almum	nurturing (Latin)
alswa	as
alta	heights
alysde	released
amen	amen
amor	love (Latin)
an	a, on, one
ana	alone
anbre	bucket
and	and
andan	injury
anes	a
angolsexna	of the Old Englishs
animæ	souls (Latin)
aninga	must-do
anum	one
aquilone	the north (Latin)
arær	raise up
aræred	raise
ardor	heat (Latin)
arfesta	merciful
asolað	grows-dirty
astelidæ	established
aþecgan	to kill
attorlaþe	cock's spur grass
auctor	author (Latin)
aurnen	passed
austro	the south (Latin)
awage	away
aweox	grow
awrat	wrote

Æ, æ

Ænglisc	English
æce	eternal
æcum	eternal
æðela	noble
æðele	nobility, noble
æðelinges	noble's
æðelredes	Æthelred's
æðelum	noble
æðelwold	Aethelwold
æghwæt	everything
æhtum	possessions
ælc	every
ælcre	each

Old English Charms, Poems, and Proverbs 1 *Word List (Ænglisc to English)*

Ænglisc	English
ælfheres	Ælfhere's, Aelfhere's (name)
Ælfred	Alfred (name)
Ælfrices	Ælfric's (a name)
ælmessan	alms
ælmihtig	almighty
æminde	forgetfulness
æne	at once
æniges	any
ænigum	any
ænyg	any
ærest	first
æror	before
æt	at, from me, in
æterna	eternal (Latin)
æþele	a noble
æþeling	prince
æþelne	noble, nobler
Æþelrædes	Aethelred's (name)
æþelre	noble
æþelum	noble
Æþlmær	Æthelmaer (a name)
ætlan	intended
ætstealle	waypoint

B, b

Ænglisc	English
baðan	Bath
bæðleem	Bethlehem
bær	bore
bæteran	better
barnum	children
be	about
beadowræda	battle bandage
beaducafa	brave-warrior's
beaduwe	battle
beaga	rings
bealuleas	the innocent
bearn	children, son
bearna	children's
bearnum	children, son
beatus	blessed (Latin)
becom	came
beda	Bede
befæste	entrusted

Ænglisc	English
bega	ring
begytan	obtain
belegde	covered
bende	bound
benne	the wound, this wound
beo	be
beoð	shall be
beorgan	defend
beorht	bright
beorhte	bright
beorn	nobleman
beornas	children-of-men
beot	boast
beoþ	be
bereafod	bereft
berhge	hill
beroþor	brother
bestemed	wet
betest	the best
Bethlem	Bethlehem
bewerode	defended
bi	about
biblos	the book (Latin)
bið	be, being
biddan	ask
bidde	ask, pray
bide	pray
bideð	awaits
bilegde	covered
billum	sword
bind	bind
binnan	within
bireð	bears
biscop	bishop
bitera	bitter
biþ	be
biþeaht	surrounded
biworpen	surrounded
blac	bright
blæd	glory
blende	blinded
bliðe	joyous
bliðemod	blithe-mood
bliðmod	blithe-minded
blindne	blinded

Old English Charms, Poems, and Proverbs 1 — Word List (Ænglisc to English)

Ænglisc	English
blis	rejoicing
blission	bliss
blode	bloodied
boca	of books
bocera	writer of books
bodade	heralded
boethia	Boethius
bogum	arms
boisil	Boisil
bona	good (Latin)
bonus	a good
br	br
brada	broad
breðel	brittle
bremes	celebrated
breoma	celebrated
breome	famous
breotenrice	Britain-kingdom
bretene	Britain
brimstream	ocean-stream
britnian	dispense
britnode	bestowed
brohte	brought
broþer	brother
brymmas	waves
brytnodon	bestowed
bryttum	the Britons
bufan	above
burch	city
Burga	boroughs
burgenda	of the Burgundians
burgum	cities
burh	town
burnon	burn
burston	burst
buruh	town
butan	except, without
buton	except
byð	be
byfigynde	trembling
byre	his child
byri	city
byrig	town
byrigde	buried
byrnan.	armour
byrnende	burning
byrnhomon	armour
byscop	a bishop

C, c

Ænglisc	English
caelorum	of heaven (Latin)
can	can
cassuc	cassock
casta	chaste
cealde	cold
ceap	property
ceapa	cattle
cennan	bear
Christi	of Christ
christum	Christ (Latin)
christus	Christ (Latin)
cide	chide
cigað	call
cinges	the-king's
clænan	clean
clæne	chaste, clean
clara	clear (Latin)
clea	claw
clemens	clement (Latin)
clene	clean
clinge	shrink
cnut	Canute
cnyssan	drive
col	coal
colian	became-cold
com	came
coman	came
comon	came
consolde	comfrey
constantinus	Constantinus
corðre	assembly
cosmi	of the world (Latin)
cosmo	the world
costunga	temptation
cræftig	skilful
Crist	Christ, Christ (a name)
criste	Christ, Christ (a name), Christ (name)

Old English Charms, Poems, and Proverbs 1 *Word List (Ænglisc to English)*

Ænglisc	English	Ænglisc	English
cristes	Christ's	Dene	the-Danes
crop	sprout	deoðdaege	death-day
crucem	the cross	deope	deep
Crux	the cross, the cross (Latin)	deor	beasts
cudberch	Cuthbert	deora	deer
cudberte	Cuthbert	Deoraby	Derby
cum	with (Latin)	deore	dear, the dear
cumen	coming	derian	harm
cunne	know	deus	god (Latin)
cuþe	be able to	dile	dill
cwæð	saying	dinamis	powerful (Latin)
cweð	say	dionisius	Dionisius
cweðan	speak	diopian	deepen
cweðe	say	do	do
cwet	saying	docce	sorrel
cweþ	say	doemed	deemed
cweþe	say	doemid	deemed
Cwyð	say	dogode	for days
cyme	come	dolh	the pain
cymeð	arrives	dom	glory, judgement
cyning	king, king, king	doma	deeming
cyninga	kings	domę	glory
cyningc	king of	domes	judgement
cyninge	king	domfæstne	judgement-firm
cyninges	king, king's	Dor	The Dore
cyst	choice	dreamas	joys
		dreame	rejoicing

D, d

		dreogeð	enduring
daed	deed, deed	dreorlicre	bloodier
dæda	deeds	drihnes	Lord's
dædfruma	deed-doer	drihten	lord, the Lord
dædum	deeds	drihtne	lord
dæg	day, the day	dryctin	lord
dæge	day	dryhten	the-lord
Dæne	Danes	dryhtne	the Lord, the-lord
dagas	days	dryhtscipe	valour
dalum	dales	duguðe	goods, virtue
de	of (Latin)	dweores	the dwarf's
deað	death	dweorh	a dwarf
deaðdege	death-day	dydon	doing
deaþe	death	dydon.	did
demed	deemed	dyre	dear
dena	the Danes	dyrre	dare

Ð, ð

Old English Charms, Poems, and Proverbs 1   Word List (Ænglisc to English)

Ænglisc	English
ða	that, the, then
ðaem	the, the
ðær	that, there
ðære	there
ðæs	this
ðæt	that
ðam	that, that, the, the
ðan	the
ðara	those
ðas	this
ðe	as, of, that, the, to, to-thee, to-you, which, who, you
ðeah	though, yet
ðearf	needs
ðegen	thane
ðem	these, they
ðence	intent
ðenden	as-long-as
ðene	the
ðeoda	nations
ðeodric	Theodric
ðeos	this
ðer	there
ðere	this
ðes	these, this
ði	the, your
ðin	you, your
ðinne	your
ðis	this
ðisse	this
ðohte	thought
ðon	than
ðonne	then, when
ðonosnottorra	thought-wiser
ðreat	crowd
ðu	you
ðurh	in, through
ðus	thus
ðusend	thousand
ðy	it, that, therefore

E, e

Ænglisc	English
e	e
ea	river
eac	also, too
eadberch	Eadbert
eadelenan	Blessed-Helen (a name)
eadfrið	Eadfrid
eadgan	blessed
eadgar	Edgar
eadig	blessed
eadige	blessed
Eadmund	Eadmund, Edmund
eadmundes	Edmund's
eadwacer	Eadwacer (a name)
eadward	Edward
eadwarde	Edward
Eadweardes	Edward
eafora	descendants
eagan	eyes
eal	all
ealaþ	ale
ealdan	old
ealdelm	Aldhelm
ealdne	old
ealdor	lord
eall	all
ealle	all
ealles	all, every
eallum	all
ealne	all
ealneg	always
ealra	all
eardast	dwell
earde	land
eardiæð	inhabited
eardwica	dwelling place
eare	ear, ears
earmlice	miserably
earne	somewhere
earnes	eagle's, the eagle's
earnian	earning
earnunga	earning
eart	be
east	east
eaþe	easily
eaxelum	shoulders

94

Old English Charms, Poems, and Proverbs 1 *Word List (Ænglisc to English)*

Ænglisc	English
ec	also, other
ece	eternal, everlasting
eci	eternal
eðel	country
eðle	homeland
edwitscype	disgrace
edygled	the country
efne	even
eft	after, afterwards, again
efter	after
eglond	island
eldum	men
elehtre	lupine
Eligbyrig	Ely-in-the-Fens (place)
ellen	courage, elder
ellenrof	courageous
elles	anything-else
encratea	power-inside
end	and
ende	end
engla	Engla, English
englas	angels
engle	Angli
englum	the Angles
enne	a
eoforbrote	carline thistle
eolone	elecampane
eom	am
eonene	pass
eorðan	earth, elders', the earth
eorðe	earth
eorl	earl
eorle	earl
eorþan	earth, the earth
eorþe	earth
eow	you
eowberge	yew berry
ermig	in pain
est	is, is (Latin)
et	and, and (Latin), on
ethel	homeland
eþeles	homeland
etiam	also (Latin)

Ænglisc	English
euthenia	prosperity

F, f

Ænglisc	English
factor	maker (Latin)
fæder	father
fæger	fair
fægere	beautifully, good
fæst	fastened
fæste	fasten
fah	hostile
fareð	fares
Farones	Pharoah's
feðewigges	foot-battle
fela	many
felterre	felterry
fenminte	fen mint
fenne	by fens
feo	livestock
feogan	hating
feoh	cattle
feohtan	fighting
feola	many
feologan	become fallow
feondscipe	enmity
feondum.	his enemies
feore	life
feorhhord	soul-hoard
ferðe	spirit
fere	drive
feredon	carried
fet	foot
feta	take
fiað	let it be so
fife	five
fifela	a monster's
filius	son (Latin)
find	find
findan	find
findanne	find
findeð	finds
finit	the end
firene	sin
firum	for-men
fisca	fish

95

Old English Charms, Poems, and Proverbs 1 — Word List (Ænglisc to English)

Ænglisc	English
fleogan	fly
fleon	fleeing
floda	flood
fo	receive, take
folc	folk
folca	folk
folces	the people
foldan	earth, lands
foldu	lands
fone	take
for	because, because-of, for
forbigan	humiliate
forbugan	for-surrendering
forð	forth
forðan	because
fore	for
forealdað	grows-old
foręldit	delays
forhelan	conceal, hidden
forholen	hidden
forleosan	for-lose
forlet;	released
fornam	swept-away
forsoc	refused
forstolen	stolen
fortis	strength (Latin)
forweorp	throw
fot	foot
frætewum	ornaments
fram	from
frea	lord
frean	lord
fremaþ	acts
freodom	freedom
freolic	freely
freolice	freely, splendid
frequenter	frequently (Latin)
friclo	aid
frið	peace
frigesscit	grows-cold (Latin)
friþes	peace
froda	wise
frofre	satisfaction
from	away, from
fruma	creator
fugle	bird
fuit	he was (Latin)
ful	full
fultum	comfort
fultumes	eagerly
fulwiht	baptism
funde	found
fundian	forwards
furðor	further
fylgan	pursued
fylste	support
fyrde	army
fyrenlice	savagely

G, g

Ænglisc	English
ga	let
gæste	ghost
gahwem	undertaking
galdor	chant
gangan	walking
garmund	Garmund (a name)
gast	spirit
gastae	spirit, spirit
gaste	spirit, spirit
ge	you
geador	together
geændade	interceded
gealdor	chant
geanoðe	meeting
geapneb	cleverly-woven
gearo	ready
geatwum	trappings
gebegde	bowed
gebide	abide, look
geboren	born
gebroþor	brethren
gebundenne	bound
gebyrd	birth
gebyrdtide	the-birth
gebyrede	birth
gecheðe	youth
gecwæð	said
gecyðed	well-known
gecyrre	turn

Old English Charms, Poems, and Proverbs 1 Word List (Ænglisc to English)

Ænglisc	English	Ænglisc	English
geðenceð.	considers	gemonge	together
gedidon	did	gemynde	mindful
gedige	prosper	gemyndi	mindful
gedo	do	gen	yet
gedon	done	genam	seized, taken
gedreas	fell	genom	took
gedreosan	perish	Geo	once
gedydon	did	geoce	support
geeode	conquered	geomres	mournful
gefeoh	rejoice	geond	around, over
geferan	companions	geong	the young
geferes	associates	geonges	youth's
gefrege	noted	georne	eagerly
gefremede	prevail	geornor	gladly
gefremian	accomplish	gerædde	advisement
gegaderod	gathered	gerimes	number, numbered
gegirwan	adorned	gesæd	spoken
gehalgod	consecrated	gesælða	of peace
gehealdan	hold	gesawe	saw
gehende	close-by	gesceaft	world
gehet	had	gesceap	creation
gehicgenne	think	gesceop	created, made
gehided.	hidden	gescyred	alloted
gehwæs	each	gesette	composed
gehwam	every	gesomnad	together
gehwilc	each	gestaðolad	founded
gehwilce	every	geswicað	abandon
gehwilces	matters	geswiceð	fail
gehwylcre	works	get	agreed
gehyded	concealed	geteled	reckoned
gehyrest	hear	geþafode	permitted
gelæde	leads	geþancie	thank
gelamp	happened	geþeoh	thrive
geleafa	faith	geþohte	thought
gelette	hindered	geþungen	gracefully
gelicade	likened	getwæmde	separate
gelifeð	trusts	geunne	grant
gelyfenne	believe	gewæxen	grown
gemæne	universal	geweald	domain
gemærsod	made famous, made-famous	geweorðad	give worthiness to
gemearcian	to-mark	geweorðod	adorned
gemetað	meet with	geweornie	wither away
gemiltsað	have mercy	gewexen	grown
gemind	thoughts	geworden	agreed, became
gemindige	mindful	gewritu	writings

97

Ænglisc	English	Ænglisc	English
gewurðað	being	hafa	have
gewurþe	become	hafað	has
giedd	poem	hagenan	Hagen's
gief	give	hagestealde	young and brave
gif	if	haleg	holy
gife	a gift	halewæge	the hallows
gifeðe	given	halgad	hallowed
gihuaes	each	halgan	holy, holy one
gioce	support	halgungboc	holy-book
gleaw	learned	halig	holy
gleawra	skilful	haligan	holy
god	god, good	haligne	holy
godaes	good	ham	home
gode	god, God (name)	haman	horse-collar
godes	God-heathen's, God's, good, wellbeing	hamelode	mutilated
		hand	hand
God's	God's	handa	hand, hands
godum	good	handwurmes	hand-worm's
Godwine	Godwin (name)	Haraldes	Harald (name)
golde	gold	hare	grey
greot	earth	harolde	Harold
gripe	gripped	hat	heat
guðbilla	battle-bill	hattæ	is named
Guðhere	Guthere's (name)	hatte	named
gy	yet	hauest	have
gyddode	spoke	he	he, it
gyf	if	heaðuwerigan	battle-weary
gyfe	gave	heafde	face
gyt	still	heafud	head
		heahþungenum	high-ranking
		heald	hold
		healde	hold
		healfe	half

H, h

Ænglisc	English	Ænglisc	English
habbanne	have	heap	pile
habben	have	heard	bitter
hæfde	had	heardne	hard-warrior
hæft	captivity	heben	heaven
hæfteclommum	binding-chains	hefaenricaes	heaven-kingdom's
hæleða	saviour	hellfirena	hell-fire-like
hæligwæter	holy water	helme	shield
hælon	covering, hit	helpe	help
hæncgest	horse	helpend	help
hærran	lord	helpes	for help
hæþenra	heathen	heo	she
hættode	scalped	heofon	heaven

Old English Charms, Poems, and Proverbs 1 | *Word List (Ænglisc to English)*

Ænglisc	English
heofonrices	heaven-kingdom's
heofonum	heaven
heolstre	dark
heom	with them
heonengange	from-here-goes
heonon	from-here
heortan	heart
heorþe	hearth
heowun	hew
her	here
hergan	honour
herigean	honour
herod	Herod (a name)
het	commanded, ordered
hi	it, the, they
hider	here
hie	he
hilde	battle
hildefrofre	weapon
him	he, him, his, is he, it, the, to-him
hine	he, him, they
hiniongae	from-here-goes
hinionge	from-here-goes
hire	these
his	he, his
hit	he, it, of it, this
hlaf	bread
hlaford	lord
hlafurd	lord
hleo	protecting
hleoðrode	spoke
ho	hang
holdlice	graciously, loyally
hoppettan	throb
hordfate	vessel
hordlocan	hoard-lock
hreowlice	cruelly
hrofe	a roof, a-roof
huaet	what-of
Humbra	Humber
hun	hundred
hund	hundred
hupeban	hipbone
huru	surely, truly
husa	houses

Ænglisc	English
hwa	who
hwæt	hear, indeed, what, what-of
hwæþre	however
hwelp	a cub
hweorfað	turn
hwet	what-of
hwilcne	which
hwile	while
hwilum	sometimes
hwit	white
Hwitanwyllesgeat	Whitwell Gap
hworfan	turn
hwylce	such
hy	he, they
hyge	mind, soul
hyne	him
hyra	their
hyrde	encouraged, heard, obeyed
hyrdes	keeper
hyrdon	obeyed
hys	his
hyt	it

I, i

Ænglisc	English
iamiamque	right now (Latin)
Ic	I
iege	island
igbuend	islanders
ige	the island
III	three-times
in	in, into, the-chamber
inn	in
innan	into, within
inne	in
inswiden	singed
inuenta	found, found (Latin)
iohannes	Iohannes
ipselos	high (Latin)
is	is, it is, that are
Iudeas	Judas
iudex	judge (Latin)
iulean	reward

Ænglisc	English
iustus	just (Latin)

K, k

Ænglisc	English
kingc	the king
kinge	king
kyn	kinds
kyneþrymme	royal-power
kyng	king
kyningc	a king
kynn	kin
kystum	of virtues

L, l

Ænglisc	English
labor	work
lac	offered
lace	offer
lacnað	healed
ladigan	excuse
laðra	foes
læcedome	remedy
lædde	led
læne	loaned
læt	allow, let
laf	legacy
lafe	remain
land	land
lande	land, of land
landes	land
lange	long
langne	long
lara	learning
lata	slack
laþ	loathsome
leaf	a leaf, leaf
lean	reward
leas	false, less
leg	lays
legde	laid
legge	lay
lende	landed
leng	longer
leo	lion

Ænglisc	English
leode	people
leodum	the people
leof	love
leofan	love
leoht	light
leohta	light
leohtes	light
lerde	learned
lesse	smaller
lice	body
lif	life
life	life
lifgende	living
Ligoraceaster	Leicester
lilie	lily
Lincylene	Lincoln
linsetcorn	linseed
litel	little
liþan	journey
liþu	limbs
locian	to look
lofe	love
longe	for a long time
losod	lost
loue	love
luce	light (Latin)
lufianne	love
lungre	suddenly
lustum	joyfully
lux	light (Latin)
lyfode	lived
lytle	little

M, m

Ænglisc	English
ma	greater, more
maðelode	spoke
madma	treasures
maðma	treasure
mæcgea	kinsmen
maecti	might
mædenman	maiden
mæg	kinsman, may, may be
mægeð	maiden

Old English Charms, Poems, and Proverbs 1   *Word List (Ænglisc to English)*

Ænglisc	English
mægen	strengths
mægenum	power
mæl	measure
mænigo	many
mæra	famous
mære	distinguished, famous
mæst	most
magna	great (Latin)
malchus	Malchus
man	a man, man, men, one
manega	many
manegum	many
manna	men
mannes	man's, person's
marian	Mary
martimianus	Martimianus
marubie	marrabulum
maximianus	Maximianus
me	me, mine, on me, to me
meahte	might
mearce	limit
mec	I
mece	Sword
mecum	sword
meder	mother
men	men
menn	man, men
meotod	creator
meotodes	the-measurer's
meridie	the south
merscmealwan	marshmallow
meteliste	food-lacking
metes	food
metod	creator, the-creator
metode	the-Creator, the-Creator
metudæs	the-measurer's
miccli	much
micel	great, many, much
micelan	great
miclum	great
micro	little (Latin)
mid	among, with
midd	the middle, with
middangeard	middle-earth
middungeard	middle-earth
mihta	might, mighty, powers
mihtan	might
mihte	might
mihton	might
mihtum	might
milde	merciful, mild
Mimming	Mimming (name)
min	mine, my
mine	of mind
mines	mine, my
minum	mine
minstre	ministers
mislice	various-ways
mod	heart, mood
modes	mind's
modgeþanc	mind-plans
modgidanc	mind-plans
modhwatu	strong souled
modsefan	spirit
moldan	top-of-the-head
mon	one, someone
moncynnæs	mankind's
moncynne	mankind
moncynnes	mankind's
monia	many
monig	many
monige	many
monna	man
monnes	man's
monnum	mankind
moste	be able to
motan	be allowed to
moten	may
mundbora	guardian
mundcræftas	protection-powers
mundi	of the world (Latin), the world's (Latin)
mundum	the world (Latin)
muneca	monk
munecon	monks
murn	fear
murnende	mournful
mycel	much
myrce	Mercia

Old English Charms, Poems, and Proverbs 1 — Word List (Ænglisc to English)

Ænglisc	English

N, n

Ænglisc	English
n	(name)
næbbe	not-have
næfre	never
næglas	nails
næni	none
naenig	none
nænige	none
næs	by-no-means
nales	never
nalles	not at all, not-at-all
nama	name
naman	names
namon	took
nanuht	nothing
nat	not
nawiht	nothing
ne	do not, does not, neither, nor, not, was-not, will-not
neah	nigh
nearwum	captivity
nedfere	needed-journey
neidfaerae	needed-journey
nemnað	name
nemnaþ	name
nenig	none
nenne	any
nergend	saviour
niða	murmuring
niðhades	Nithad's
niðweorca	conflict
nigon	nine
nihgan	next
nihtum	nights
nim	take
niman	take
nioþo	from below
niþer	downwards
niþþa	men
nitor	shining (Latin)
noma	the name
non	not (Latin)
norð	north
Norðmannum	Northmen
north	north
Nu	now
nusquam	never (Latin)
nyde	subjected

O, o

Ænglisc	English
obtenebrescit	grows-dark (Latin)
occidente	the west, the west (Latin)
oððe	or
oðehtian	disposess
oðer	of
oðfeorrganne	drive-away
oðfergean	drive-away
oðferie	drive-off
oðhealde	keep-away
oðlædanne	lead-off
oðlæde	lead-off
oðre	another
oðres	another, other
oðrum	another
oðþæt	until
oðwyrceanne	destroy
of	from, of
ofer	over
ofercom	overcame
oferfæðmed	covered
oferweorp	throw down
ofgeot	soak
oflætan	wafer, wafers
ofrað	offertory
ofsloh	slayed
oft	often
oftor	often
oliccan	praise
omnes	all (Latin)
omnia	everything (Latin)
on	about, in, of, on, over
onbere	withers
ond	and
ondred	dreaded
onette	hasten

Old English Charms, Poems, and Proverbs 1 Word List (Ænglisc to English)

Ænglisc	English
onfo	receive
ongalan	recite
ongan	undertook
ongunn	undertake
ongunnan	began
ongynnað	assail
onsended	sent
onsendon	to send
onstealde	established
op	out of
or	origin
orbem	the world (Latin)
ordfruma	creator
ordwyga	warrior
oretmægcum	warriors
orf	cattle
oriente	the east, the east (Latin)
osuualdes	Oswald's
oþ	until
oþer	other
oþerre	another
oþre	the-other
oþþe	or

P, p

Ænglisc	English
pacis	of peace (Latin)
partu	birth
pentecostenes	Pentecost
per	by
perhennem	perpetual
pleno	full (Latin)
polleie	pennyroyal
polorum	of the poles (Latin)
pondus	weight (Latin)
ponus	work (Latin)
preosta	priests

Q, q

Ænglisc	English
que	which (Latin)
quem	who (Latin)
qui	who (Latin)

R, r

Ænglisc	English
ræda	counsel
rædfæst	righteous
rædfest	sound
reaf	vestment
recce	cares-for
recon	ready
redemptor	redeemer (Latin)
reducað	is led (Latin)
reducant	led
reducat	is led (Latin), led
regem	the king (Latin)
regentem	ruling (Latin)
regit	rules (Latin)
regna	kingdom (Latin)
reliquia	relics
renig	rainy
reotugu	mournfully
restað	rest
reþehygdig	right-thinking
rhyta	rights
rice	kingdom
ricne	a-powerful
rimde	the host
rime	counted
rimes	counted
Rod	cross
rode	cross
rodores	the heavens
rogo	pray (Latin)
rume	roomy
rumre	wide
ryhte	properly

S, s

Ænglisc	English
sæt	sat, settled
saga	tell
salus	salvation (Latin)
sanctæ	holy (Latin)
sancte	saint
sancti	the saints (Latin)

Old English Charms, Poems, and Proverbs 1 — Word List (Ænglisc to English)

Ænglisc	English	Ænglisc	English
sanctus	saintly	seo	be, his, it, the
saul	soul	seoce	a sickness
saule	soul	seofon	seven
sawla	souls	serafion	Serafion
sawle	soul	sette	set
scadeþ	borders	sexum	the Saxons
scan	shining	siae	to-be
sceal	shall, should	sibbe	joys
scealt	shall	siblufan	love
sceððan	harm	sie	to-be
sceop	created, poet	siex	six
scepen	shaper	sigað	sink
scerne	dung	sige	victory
scine	shines	sigewif	victorious-women
scolde	should	sigisiþa	successful
scop	created	sigora	victories
scottum	the Scots	simle	ever
screoda	numbered	sinc	riches
scring	shrivel	sindon	they are
sculon	shall-we	sing	sing
scurum	storms	singalan	continuously
scylde	fault	singan	sing
scylun	shall-we	sinum	his
scyndeð	surged	siþþan	afterwards, thenceforth
scype	ship		
scyppend	shaper	siþum	afterwards
se	he, so, the, who	sitte	sit
sealde	sold	snotera	wiser
searohæbbendra	armoured	Snotingaham	Nottingham
secan	seek, to-seek	soð	truly
secg	warrior	soðfæst	truth-firm
secgað	say	soðfæsta	truth-fastened
secgan	tell, told	soðfæstan	truth-fastened
secge	says	soðum	true
sedentem	sitting on (Latin)	sohtest	sought
seggeð	say	sona	as soon, at once, soon
sel	better		
selast	excellence	soþfæste	righteous
seldcymas	seldom-coming	squalescit	grows-dirty (Latin)
self	himself	stæl	place of
selfne	yourself	stanas	stones
selfum	himself	standeð	stands
sende	sent	stanfate	jewelled-sheath
senescunt	grows-old (Latin)	Stanford	Stamford
sensu	sense (Latin)	steppa	steps
		stille	quietly

Old English Charms, Poems, and Proverbs 1 *Word List (Ænglisc to English)*

Ænglisc	English
stode	stood
stolenne	stolen
streawbergean	strawberry
stronge	strong
styple	steeple
suð	south
suðportice	south-porch
sue	as
sume	some, some-of
summi	highest (Latin)
summo	highest (Latin)
summus	highest (Latin)
sumum	a-certain
sunt	they, they-are (Latin)
sunu	son
supplex	supplicant (Latin)
swa	as, so, thus
swatfag	blood-stained
sweartra	darkness
swefan	death-sleep
swegles	heaven's
sweoran	neck
sweordplegan	sword-play
sweordwund	sword-wounded
sweostar	sister
swiðe	exceedingly, very-much
swiðre	right
swirman	swarming
swiþran	right
swor	swore
swurde	sword
swylce	likewise, such, such as
swyltit	dies
sy	be, is, to-be
Syððan	afterwards, since
syle	give
sylfan	his-self
sylfum	himself
syllan	give
symle	always, forever
syncfatum	precious-treasures
synna	sin
syre	rotten
syþþan	since

T, t

Ænglisc	English
talade	numbered
teage	ties
tearige	teary
tenet	holds (Latin)
teode	titled
teorað	fail
throno	thrones
thronum	the throne
tiadæ	titled
tid	a time, time
tiid	time
til	for
timbrien	build
tireadge	glorious
to	for, forth, go to, in, to, too
todraf	destroyed
torhte	bright
toscufeð	do-away
tosliteð	tears-apart
toward	toward
treowe	faith
treowgeþofta	trusted-friends
treowum	trees
tun	dwelling
tungan	tongue
twega	two-things
twentig	twenty
tyn	ten

Þ, þ

Ænglisc	English
þa	as, being, that, the, then, then, when, yet
þæm	that, the, they
þæne	the
þænne	then
þær	there
þære	to the
þæs	because, of-that, so, that, the, this

Old English Charms, Poems, and Proverbs 1 — Word List (Ænglisc to English)

Ænglisc	English
þæt	that, the
þætte	that
þam	that, the, the, them, then
þan	than, the
þance	thank
þances	thought
þar	there
þarf	needs
þas	these, this, this
þe	any, as, for you, however, it, that, the, then, though, which, who, you
þeah	nevertheless, though
þearf	necessary, needs
þeh	though
þence	intend, think
þenden	so long as
þeoda	nations
þeoden	lord, the-lord
þeodkyninges	great-king
þeodne	the prince
þeos	this
þer	there
þet	that
þi	therefore
þin	your
þine	to you, your
þinga	thing
þingian	intercede
þinne	your
þinre	your, yours
þinum	your, yours
þis	it, this
þison	this
þon	from there, that, then
þoncsnotturra	thought-wiser
þone	the, then, those
þonne	from there, from-there, than, then, there, those, when, whenever, whereby
þrage	for a time, for-a-time
þreat	a troop
þriwa	three times, three-times
þry	three
þrym	three
þrymcyningc	the ruling king
þu	you
þureð	Thureth
þurh	by, for the sake of, sake-of, through
þus	thus
þy	by this
þyos	this
þystel	thistle
þystre	darkness

U, u

Ænglisc	English
uard	ward
uerc	work-of
ueþer	wing
uirginem	the virgin (Latin)
uirginis	maiden (Latin)
uirtute	virtue (Latin)
uiuendo	living (Latin)
unarimeda	unnumbered
uncer	our
uncerne	ours
uncuþ	unknowing
under	under
ungelic	unlike
ungelice	unlike
ungerim	innumerable
unica	one (Latin)
unmægas	unrelated
unriht	un-right
unryhte	un-right
unsceððiga	innocent
unscende	blameless
uoca	call (Latin)
uoce	voice (Latin)
uoluntate	will (Latin)
urne	our
us	to us, upon us, us
userne	ours
usic	us
ussum	us
ut	out

Old English Charms, Poems, and Proverbs 1 — Word List (Ænglisc to English)

Ænglisc	English
uton	let us
uuldurfadur	glory-father
uundra	wonder

V, v

Ænglisc	English
vii	seven

W, w

Ænglisc	English
waciaþ	awaken
wælreowe	bloodthirsty
wæra	keeping
wæran	were
wære	was, were
wæron	were
wæs	to be, was
wæterælfadle	water elf disease
wætre	water
waldend	ruler
waldere	Waldere
walum	the Welsh
wat	know
waxsian	grow
we	we
weal	the-wall
wealdan	rule over, wielded
wealdend	ruler
weallendan	welling
weard	keep, ward
wearð	became, worthy
weder	weather
wel	well
welan	wealth
Welande	Weland's (name)
welandes	Weland's
wena	hopes
wenchichenne	little wen
wendest	expected
wene	think
wenne	wen
wenum	hopes
weolan	wealth
weold	ruling
weoldon	ruled
weor	the Wear
weorc	work-of
weorcum	work
weorða	worthiness
weorðae	of-worth
weorðmynda	worth-minded
weorne	evaporate
weornie	waste-away
weornige	waste-away
weorþe	of-worth
weorþscipe	worthship
weorudes	troops
weox	waxed
wer	man
wera	man, of man
weras	men
wereð	protects
wereda	army
wermod	wormwood
wes	was
west	west
westende	west-end
weter	water
wið	against
widan	wide
wiððon	afterwards
wide	wide, widely
widia	Widia
widian	to Widia
widlastum	far-wandering
wig	battle
wiga	warrior
wiggendra	warriors
wigrædenne	warfare
wiht	creature
wihta	beings
wihte	anything
wilda	wild
wilde	wild
wile	willing
willa	will
willað	will
Wincestre	Winchester (place)
wine	friend

107

Old English Charms, Poems, and Proverbs 1 — Word List (Ænglisc to English)

Ænglisc	English
wintergeteles	winters-numbered
wintra	winters
wiorðe.	of-worth
wiorðeð	will-be
witanne	protect
wiurðit	will-be
wlance	the proud
wlite	beauty
wolde	wished
wolues	the wolf's
wonne	dark
worc	work
word	word
wordbeot	word-vows
worde	word
wordum	words
woruld	world
worulda	the world
worulde	the-world
woruldrice	world-kingdom
wræclastum	outcast
wraþe	wrathfully
writ	writings
writan	write
wuda	the woods
wudafæstern	wood-fastened
wudu	wood
wuldor	glory
wuldorfæder	glory-father
wuldres	glory, wondrous
wulf	Wulf (a name)
wulfes	to Wulf (a name)
wunað	dwell
wund	wound
wunde	wounds
wundorlicne	wondrous
wundra	wonder
wundrum	wondrous, wondrously
wuniad	live
wunian	dwelling
wunode	dwelled, dwelt
wurðe	worth
wurðlice	worthiness
wurðmynt	honour
wurþe	become
wycum	dwellings
wyle	wishes
wyn	delight
wynstre	left
wyrcean	created
wyrde	destroyed
wyrðe	become, worthy
wyrican	made
wyrrestan	worst
wyrstan	worst
wyrþe	become
wyrþeþ	will-be

X, x

Ænglisc	English
xx	twenty
xxiiii	twenty four
xxviii	twenty-eight
xxx	thirty

Y, y

Ænglisc	English
yðum	waves
yfel	badly, evil
yfeles	evil
yfla	evil
yflaes	evil
yfles	evil
ymbclyppað	embraced
ymbe	a swarm of bees
ymbeornad	beholds
ymbhycgenne	about-think
ymbhycggannae	about-think
ymbutan	about
yþ	wave

Word List *(English to Ænglisc)*

English	Ænglisc	English	Ænglisc
		Akeman's Town	acemannesceastre
		Aldhelm	ealdelm
A, a		*ale*	ealaþ
		Alfred (name)	Ælfred
a	a, an, anes, enne	*all*	a, eal, eall, ealle, ealles, eallum, ealne, ealra
a bishop	byscop		
a cub	hwelp		
a dwarf	dweorh		
a gift	gife	*all (Latin)*	omnes
a good	bonus	*alloted*	gescyred
a king	kyningc	*allow*	læt
a leaf	leaf	*almighty*	ælmihtig, allmectig
a man	man	*alms*	ælmessan
a monster's	fifela	*alone*	ana
a noble	æþele	*also*	eac, ec
a roof	hrofe	*also (Latin)*	etiam
a sickness	seoce	*always*	a, ealneg, symle
a swarm of bees	ymbe	*am*	eom
a time	tid	*amen*	amen
a troop	þreat	*among*	mid
abandon	geswicað	*and*	and, end, et, ond
abbot	abbot	*and (Latin)*	et
abide	gebide	*angels*	englas
about	be, bi, on, ymbutan	*Angli*	engle
about-think	ymbhycgenne, ymbhycggannae	*another*	oðre, oðres, oðrum, oþerre
above	bufan	*any*	æniges, ænigum, ænyg, nenne, þc
accomplish	gefremian		
a-certain	sumum	*anything*	wihte
achieve	agan	*anything-else*	elles
acts	fremaþ	*a-powerful*	ricne
adorned	gegirwan, geweorðod	*armour*	byrnan., byrnhomon
advisement	gerædde	*armoured*	searohæbbendra
Aelfhere's (name)	ælfheres	*arms*	bogum
Aethelred's (name)	Æþelrædes	*army*	fyrde, wereda
Aethelwold	æðelwold	*a-roof*	hrofe
after	aefter, æfter, eft, efter	*around*	geond
afterwards	eft, siþþan, siþum, Syððan, widðon	*arrives*	cymeð
		as	alswa, ðe, sue, swa, þa, þe
again	eft		
against	wið	*as soon*	sona
agreed	get, geworden	*ask*	biddan, bidde
aid	friclo	*as-long-as*	ðenden
Aidan	aidan	*assail*	ongynnað
		assembly	corðre

109

Old English Charms, Poems, and Proverbs 1 — Word List (English to Ænglisc)

English	Ænglisc
associates	geferes
at	æt
at once	æne, sona
author (Latin)	auctor
awaits	bideð
awaken	waciaþ
away	awage, from

Æ, æ

English	Ænglisc
Ælfhere's	ælfheres
Ælfric's (a name)	Ælfrices
Æthelmaer (a name)	Æþlmær
Æthelred's	æðelredes
Æthelwold (a name)	Aðelwold

B, b

English	Ænglisc
badly	yfel
baptism	fulwiht
Bath	baðan
battle	beaduwe, hilde, wig
battle bandage	beadowræda
battle-bill	guðbilla
battle-weary	heaðuwerigan
be	beo, beoþ, bið, biþ, byð, eart, seo, sy
be able to	cuþe, moste
be allowed to	motan
bear	cennan
bears	bireð
beasts	deor
beautifully	fægere
beauty	wlite
became	geworden, wearð
became-cold	colian
because	for, forðan, þæs
because-of	for
become	gewurþe, wurþe, wyrðe, wyrþe
become fallow	feologan
becomes-loathed	alaðaþ
Bede	beda
before	aer, ær, æror
began	ongunnan
beholds	ymbeornad
being	bið, gewurðað, þa
beings	wihta
believe	gelyfenne
bereft	bereafod
bestowed	britnode, brytnodon
Bethlehem	bæðleem, Bethlem
better	bæteran, sel
bind	bind
binding-chains	hæfteclommum
bird	fugle
birth	gebyrd, gebyrede, partu
bishop	biscop
bitter	bitera, heard
blameless	unscende
blessed	eadgan, eadig, eadige
blessed (Latin)	beatus
Blessed-Helen (a name)	eadelenan
blinded	blende, blindne
bliss	blission
blithe-minded	bliðmod
blithe-mood	bliðemod
bloodied	blode
bloodier	dreorlicre
blood-stained	swatfag
bloodthirsty	wælreowe
boast	beot
body	lice
Boethius	boethia
Boisil	boisil
borders	scadeþ
bore	bær
born	acenned, geboren
boroughs	Burga
bound	bende, gebundenne
bowed	gebegde
br	br
brave-warrior's	beaducafa
bread	hlaf
brethren	gebroþor
bright	beorht, beorhte, blac, torhte

110

Old English Charms, Poems, and Proverbs 1   *Word List (English to Ænglisc)*

English	Ænglisc
Britain	bretene
Britain-kingdom	breotenrice
brittle	breðel
broad	brada
brother	beroþor, broþer
brought	brohte
brought-forth	acænned
bucket	anbre
build	timbrien
buried	byrigde
burn	burnon
burning	byrnende
burst	burston
but	ac
by	per, þurh
by fens	fenne
by this	þy
by-no-means	næs

C, c

English	Ænglisc
call	cigað
call (Latin)	uoca
came	becom, com, coman, comon
can	can
Canute	cnut
captivity	hæft, nearwum
cares-for	recce
carline thistle	eoforþrote
carried	feredon
cassock	cassuc
cattle	ceapa, feoh, orf
celebrated	bremes, breoma
chant	galdor, gealdor
chaste	casta, clæne
chide	cide
children	barnum, bearn, bearnum
children-of-men	beornas
children's	bearna
choice	cyst
Christ	Crist, criste
Christ (a name)	crist, Criste
Christ (Latin)	christum, christus

English	Ænglisc
Christ (name)	Criste
Christ's	cristes
cities	burgum
city	burch, byri
claw	clea
clean	clænan, clæne, clene
clear (Latin)	clara
clement (Latin)	clemens
cleverly-woven	geapneb
close-by	gehende
coal	col
cock's spur grass	attorlaþe
cold	cealde
come	cyme
comfort	fultum
comfrey	consolde
coming	cumen
commanded	het
companions	geferan
composed	gesette
conceal	forhelan
concealed	gehyded
conflict	niðweorca
conquered	geeode
consecrated	gehalgod
considers	geðenceð.
Constantinus	constantinus
continuously	singalan
counsel	ræda
counted	rime, rimes
country	eðel
courage	ellen
courageous	ellenrof
covered	belegde, bilegde, oferfæðmed
covering	hælon
created	gesceop, sceop, scop, wyrcean
creation	gesceap
creator	fruma, meotod, metod, ordfruma
creature	wiht
cross	Rod, rode
crowd	ðreat
cruelly	hreowlice
Cuthbert	cudberch, cudberte

111

Old English Charms, Poems, and Proverbs 1 Word List (English to Ænglisc)

English	Ænglisc

D, d

English	Ænglisc
dales	dalum
Danes	Dæne
dare	dyrre
dark	heolstre, wonne
darkness	sweartra, þystre
day	dæg, dæge
days	dagas
dear	deore, dyre
death	deað, deaþe
death-day	deaðdege, deoðdaege
death-sleep	swefan
deed	daed, dæd
deed-doer	dædfruma
deeds	dæda, dædum
deemed	demed, doemed, doemid
deeming	doma
deep	deope
deepen	diopian
deer	deora
defend	beorgan
defended	bewerode
delaying	agælde
delays	foreldit
delight	wyn
Derby	Deoraby
descendants	eafora
destroy	oðwyrceanne
destroyed	todraf, wyrde
did	dydon., gedidon, gedydon
dies	swyltit
dill	dile
Dionisius	dionisius
disgrace	edwitscype
dispense	britnian
disposess	oðehtian
distinguished	mære
do	do, gedo
do not	ne
do-away	toscufeð

English	Ænglisc
does not	ne
doing	dydon
domain	geweald
done	gedon
downwards	niþer
dreaded	ondred
drive	cnyssan, fere
drive-away	oðfeorrganne, oðfergean
drive-off	oðferie
dung	scerne
dwell	eardast, wunað
dwelled	wunode
dwelling	tun, wunian
dwelling place	eardwica
dwellings	wycum
dwelt	wunode

E, e

English	Ænglisc
e	e
each	ælcre, gehwæs, gehwilc, gihuaes
Eadbert	eadberch
Eadfrid	eadfrið
Eadmund	Eadmund
Eadwacer (a name)	eadwacer
eagerly	fultumes, georne
eagle's	earnes
ear	eare
earl	eorl, eorle
earning	earnian, earnunga
ears	eare
earth	eorðan, eorðe, eorþan, eorþe, foldan, greot
easily	eaþe
east	east
Edgar	eadgar
Edmund	Eadmund
Edmund's	eadmundes
Edward	eadward, eadwarde, Eadweardes
elder	ellen
elders'	aelda, eorðan

Old English Charms, Poems, and Proverbs 1

English	Ænglisc
elecampane	eolone
Ely-in-the-Fens (place)	Eligbyrig
embraced	ymbclyppað
encouraged	hyrde
end	ende
enduring	dreogeð
Engla	engla
English	engla, feondscipe
enmity	feondscipe
entrusted	befæste
established	astelidæ, onstealde
eternal	æce, æcum, ece, eci
eternal (Latin)	æterna, aeternus
evaporate	weorne
even	efne
ever	a, simle
everlasting	ece
every	ælc, ealles, gehwam, gehwilce
everything	æghwæt
everything (Latin)	omnia
evil	yfel, yfeles, yfla, yflaes, yfles
exceedingly	swiðe
excellence	selast
except	butan, buton
excuse	ladigan
expected	wendest
eyes	eagan

F, f

English	Ænglisc
face	heafde
fades-away (Latin)	abolescit
fail	geswiceð, teorað
fair	fæger
faith	geleafa, treowe
false	
famous	breome, mæra, mære
fares	fareð
far-wandering	widlastum
fasten	fæste
fastened	fæst
father	fæder

Word List (English to Ænglisc)

English	Ænglisc
fault	scylde
fear	murn
fell	gedreas
felterry	felterre
fen mint	fenminte
fighting	feohtan
find	find, findan, findanne
finds	findeð
first	ær, ærest, aerist
fish	fisca
five	fife
fleeing	fleon
flood	floda
fly	fleogan
foes	laðra
folk	folc, folca
food	metes
food-lacking	meteliste
foot	fet, fot
foot-battle	feðewigges
for	for, fore, til, to
for a long time	longe
for a time	þrage
for days	dogode
for help	helpes
for the sake of	þurh
for you	þe
for-a-time	þrage
forever	symle
forgetfulness	æminde
for-lose	forleosan
for-men	firum
for-surrendering	forbugan
forth	forð, to
forwards	fundian
found	funde, inuenta
found (Latin)	inuenta
founded	gestaðolad
freedom	freodom
freely	freolic, freolice
frequently (Latin)	frequenter
friend	wine
from	a, ab, fram, from, of
from (Latin)	ab
from below	nioþo

113

Old English Charms, Poems, and Proverbs 1   Word List (English to Ænglisc)

English	Ænglisc	English	Ænglisc
from me	æt	grey	hare
from there	þon, þonne	gripped	gripe
from-here	heonon	grow	ace, aweox, waxsian
from-here-goes	heonengange, hiniongae, hinionge	grown	gewæxen, gewexen
		grows	ace
from-there	þonne	grows-cold	acolað
full	ful	grows-cold (Latin)	frigesscit
full (Latin)	pleno	grows-dark	aðystrað
further	furðor	grows-dark (Latin)	obtenebrescit
		grows-dirty	asolað
		grows-dirty (Latin)	squalescit
		grows-old	forealdað
		grows-old (Latin)	senescunt
		guardian	mundbora
		Guthere's (name)	Guðhere

G, g

English	Ænglisc
Garmund (a name)	garmund
gathered	gegaderod
gave	gyfe
ghost	gæste
give	gief, syle, syllan
give worthiness to	geweorðad
given	gifeðe
gladly	geornor
glorious	tireadge
glory	blæd, dom, dome, wuldor, wuldres
glory-father	uuldurfadur, wuldorfæder
go to	to
god	god, gode
god (Latin)	deus
God (name)	gode
God-heathen's	godes
God's	godes, God's
Godwin (name)	Godwine
going	agangen
gold	golde
good	fægere, god, godaes, godes, godum
good (Latin)	bona
goods	duguðe
gracefully	geþungen
graciously	holdlice
grant	geunne
great	micel, micelan, miclum
great (Latin)	magna
greater	ma
great-king	þeodkyninges

H, h

English	Ænglisc
had	gehet, hæfde
Hagen's	hagenan
half	healfe
hallowed	halgad
hand	hand, handa
hands	handa
hand-worm's	handwurmes
hang	ho
hanged	ahangen
happened	gelamp
Harald (name)	Haraldes
hard-warrior	heardne
harm	derian, sceððan
Harold	harolde
has	hafað
hasten	onette
hating	feogan
have	habbanne, habben, hafa, hauest
have mercy	gemiltsað
he	he, hie, him, hine, his, hit, hy, se
he was (Latin)	fuit
head	heafud
healed	lacnað
hear	gehyrest, hwæt
heard	hyrde

Old English Charms, Poems, and Proverbs 1 *Word List (English to Ænglisc)*

English	Ænglisc
heart	heortan, mod
hearth	heorþe
heat	hat
heat (Latin)	ardor
heathen	hæþenra
heaven	heben, heofon, heofonum
heaven-kingdom's	hefaenricaes, heofonrices
heaven's	swegles
heights	alta
heir-of	afera
hell-fire-like	hellfirena
help	helpe, helpend
heralded	bodade
here	her, hider
Herod (a name)	herod
hew	heowun
hidden	forhelan, forholen, gehided.
hidden (Latin)	abscondita
high (Latin)	ipselos
highest (Latin)	summi, summo, summus
high-ranking	heahþungenum
hill	berhge
him	him, hine, hyne
himself	self, selfum, sylfum
hindered	gelette
hipbone	hupeban
his	him, his, hys, seo, sinum
his child	byre
his enemies	feondum.
his-self	sylfan
hit	hælon
hoard-lock	hordlocan
hold	gehealdan, heald, healde
holds (Latin)	tenet
holy	haleg, halgan, halig, haligan, haligne
holy (Latin)	sanctæ
holy one	halgan
holy water	hæligwæter
holy-book	halgungboc
home	ham

English	Ænglisc
homeland	eðle, ethel, eþeles
honour	hergan, herigean, wurðmynt
hopes	wena, wenum
horse	hæncgest
horse-collar	haman
hostile	fah
houses	husa
however	hwæþre, þe
Humber	Humbra
humiliate	forbigan
hundred	hun, hund
hung up	ahengon

I, i

English	Ænglisc
I	ic, mec
if	gif, gyf
in	æt, ðurh, in, inn, inne, on, to
in pain	ermig
indeed	hwæt
inhabited	eardiæð
injury	andan
innocent	unsceððiga
innumerable	ungerim
intend	þence
intended	ætlan
intent	ðence
intercede	þingian
interceded	geændade
into	in, innan
Iohannes	iohannes
is	est, is, sy
is (Latin)	est
is he	him
is led (Latin)	reducað, reducat
is named	hattæ
island	eglond, iege
islanders	igbuend
it	ðy, he, hi, him, hit, hyt, seo, þe, þis
it is	is

115

English	Ænglisc	English	Ænglisc
		lead-off	oðlædanne, oðlæde
		leads	gelæde
		leaf	leaf

J, j

English	Ænglisc
jewelled-sheath	stanfate
journey	liþan
joyfully	lustum
joyous	bliðe
joys	dreamas, sibbe
Judas	Iudeas
judge (Latin)	iudex
judgement	dom, domes
judgement-firm	domfæstne
just (Latin)	iustus

K, k

English	Ænglisc
keep	weard
keep-away	oðhealde
keeper	hyrdes
keeping	wæra
killed	acwealde
kin	kynn
kinds	kyn
king	cyning, cyninge, cyninges, kinge, kyng
king of	cyningc
king, king	cyning
kingdom	rice
kingdom (Latin)	regna
kings	cyninga
king's	cyninges
kinsman	mæg
kinsmen	mæcgea
know	cunne, wat

L, l

English	Ænglisc
laid	legde
land	earde, land, lande, landes
landed	lende
lands	foldan, foldu
lay	legge
lays	leg

English	Ænglisc
learned	gleaw, lerde
learning	lara
led	lædde, reducant, reducat
left	wynstre
legacy	laf
Leicester	Ligoraceaster
less	leas
let	ga, læt
let it be so	fiað
let us	uton
life	feore, lif, life
light	leoht, leohta, leohtes
light (Latin)	luce, lux
likened	gelicade
likewise	swylce
lily	lilie
limbs	liþu
limit	mearce
Lincoln	Lincylene
linseed	linsetcorn
lion	leo
little	litel, lytle
little (Latin)	micro
little wen	wenchichenne
live	wuniad
lived	lyfode
livestock	feo
living	lifgende
living (Latin)	uiuendo
loaned	læne
loathsome	laþ
long	lange, langne
longer	leng
look	gebide
lord	drihten, drihtne, dryctin, ealdor, frea, frean, hærran, hlaford, hlafurd, þeoden
Lord's	drihnes
lost	losod

Old English Charms, Poems, and Proverbs 1 — Word List (English to Ænglisc)

English	Ænglisc
love	leof, leofan, lofe, loue, lufianne, siblufan
love (Latin)	amor
loyally	holdlice
lupine	elehtre

M, m

English	Ænglisc
made	gesceop, wyrican
made famous	gemærsod
made-famous	gemærsod
maiden	mædenman, mægeð
maiden (Latin)	uirginis
maker (Latin)	factor
Malchus	malchus
man	man, menn, monna, wer, wera
mankind	moncynne, monnum
mankind's	moncynnæs, moncynnes
man's	mannes, monnes
many	fela, feola, mænigo, manega, manegum, micel, monia, monig, monige
marrabulum	marubie
marshmallow	merscmealwan
Martimianus	martimianus
Mary	marian
matters	gehwilces
Maximianus	maximianus
may	mæg, moten
may be	mæg
me	me
measure	mæl
meet with	gemetað
meeting	geanoðe
men	eldum, man, manna, men, menn, niþþa, weras
Mercia	myrce
merciful	arfesta, milde
middle-earth	middangeard, middungeard
might	maecti, meahte, mihta, mihtan, mihte, mihton, mihtum
mighty	mihta
mild	milde
Mimming (name)	Mimming
mind	hyge
mindful	gemindige, gemynde, gemyndi
mind-plans	modgeþanc, modgidanc
mind's	modes
mine	me, min, mines, minum
ministers	minstre
miserably	earmlice
monk	muneca
monks	munecon
mood	mod
more	ma
most	mæst
mother	meder
mournful	geomres, murnende
mournfully	reotugu
much	miccli, micel, mycel
murmuring	niða
must-do	aninga
mutilated	hamelode
my	min, mines

N, n

English	Ænglisc
nails	næglas
name	nama, nemnað, nemnaþ
named	hatte
names	naman
nations	ðeoda, þeoda
necessary	þearf
neck	sweoran
needed-journey	nedfere, neidfaerae
needs	ðearf, þarf, þearf
neither	ne
never	næfre, nales
never (Latin)	nusquam
nevertheless	ac, þeah

117

Old English Charms, Poems, and Proverbs 1 — Word List (English to Ænglisc)

English	Ænglisc
next	nihgan
nigh	neah
nights	nihtum
nine	nigon
Nithad's	niðhades
nobility	æðele
noble	æðela, æðele, æðelum, æþelne, æþelre, æþelum
nobleman	beorn
nobler	æþelne
noble's	æðelinges
none	næni, naenig, nænige, nenig
nor	ne
north	norð, north
Northmen	Norðmannum
not	nat, ne
not (Latin)	non
not at all	nalles
not-at-all	nalles
noted	gefrege
not-have	næbbe
nothing	nanuht, nawiht
Nottingham	Snotingaham
now	Nu
number	gerimes
numbered	gerimes, screoda, talade
nurturing (Latin)	almum

O, o

English	Ænglisc
oaths	aðas
obeyed	hyrde, hyrdon
obtain	begytan
ocean-stream	brimstream
of	ðe, oðer, of, on
of (Latin)	de
of books	boca
of Christ	Christi
of heaven (Latin)	caelorum
of it	hit
of land	lande
of man	wera
of mind	mine
of peace	gesælða
of peace (Latin)	pacis
of the Anglo-Saxons	angolsexna
of the Burgundians	burgenda
of the poles (Latin)	polorum
of the world (Latin)	cosmi, mundi
of virtues	kystum
offer	lace
offered	lac
offertory	ofrað
often	oft, oftor
of-that	þæs
of-worth	weorðae, weorþe, wiorðe.
old	ealdan, ealdne
on	an, et, on
on me	me
once	Geo
one	an, anum, man, mon
one (Latin)	unica
or	aeðða, oððe, oþþe
ordered	het
origin	or
ornaments	frætewum
Oswald's	osuualdes
other	ec, oðres, oþer
our	uncer, urne
ours	uncerne, userne
out	ut
out of	op
outcast	wræclastum
over	geond, ofer, on
overcame	ofercom
own	age

P, p

English	Ænglisc
pass	eonene
passed	aurnen
peace	frið, friþes
pennyroyal	polleie
Pentecost	pentecostenes
people	leode
perish	gedreosan

Old English Charms, Poems, and Proverbs 1 — Word List (English to Ænglisc)

English	Ænglisc	English	Ænglisc
permitted	geþafode	redeemer (Latin)	redemptor
perpetual	perhennem	refused	forsoc
person's	mannes	rejoice	gefeoh
Pharoah's	Farones	rejoicing	blis, dreame
pile	heap	released	alysde, forlet;
place of	stæl	relics	reliquia
poem	giedd	remain	lafe
poet	sceop	remedy	læcedome
possessions	æhtum	rest	restað
power	mægenum	reward	iulean, lean
powerful (Latin)	dinamis	riches	sinc
power-inside	encratea	right	swiðre, swiþran
powers	mihta	right now (Latin)	iamiamque
praise	oliccan	righteous	rædfæst, soþfæste
pray	bidde, bide	rights	rhyta
pray (Latin)	rogo	right-thinking	reþehygdig
precious-treasures	syncfatum	ring	bega
prevail	gefremede	rings	beaga
priests	preosta	river	ea
prince	æþeling	roomy	rume
properly	ryhte	rotten	syre
property	ceap	royal-power	kyneþrymme
prosper	gedige	rule over	wealdan
prosperity	euthenia	ruled	weoldon
protect	witanne	ruler	waldend, wealdend
protecting	hleo	rules (Latin)	regit
protection-powers	mundcræftas	ruling	weold
protects	wereð	ruling (Latin)	regentem
pursued	fylgan		

Q, q

English	Ænglisc
quenched	adwæsce
quietly	stille

R, r

English	Ænglisc
rainy	renig
raise	aræred
raise up	arær
ready	gearo, recon
receive	fo, onfo
recite	ongalan
reckoned	geteled

S, s

English	Ænglisc
said	gecwæð
saint	sancte
saintly	sanctus
sake-of	þurh
salvation (Latin)	salus
sat	sæt
satisfaction	frofre
savagely	fyrenlice
saviour	hæleða, nergend
saw	gesawe
say	cweð, cweðe, cweþ, cweþe, Cwyð, secgað, seggeð
saying	cwæð, cwet

Old English Charms, Poems, and Proverbs 1 — Word List (English to Ænglisc)

English	Ænglisc
says	secge
scalped	hættode
seek	secan
seized	genam
seldom-coming	seldcymas
sense (Latin)	sensu
sent	onsended, sende
separate	getwæmde
Serafion	serafion
set	sette
settled	sæt
seven	seofon, vii
shall	sceal, scealt
shall be	beoð
shall-we	sculon, scylun
shaper	scepen, scyppend
she	heo
shield	helme
shines	scine
shining	scan
shining (Latin)	nitor
ship	scype
should	sceal, scolde
shoulders	eaxelum
shrink	clinge
shrivel	scring
sick-person	adlegan
sin	firene, synna
since	syððan, syþþan
sing	sing, singan
singed	inswiden
sink	sigað
sister	sweostar
sit	sitte
sitting on (Latin)	sedentem
six	siex
skilful	cræftig, gleawra
slack	lata
slayed	ofsloh
smaller	lesse
so	ac, se, swa, þæs
so long as	þenden
soak	ofgeot
sold	sealde
some	sume
some-of	sume
someone	mon
sometimes	hwilum
somewhere	earne
son	bearn, bearnum, sunu
son (Latin)	filius
soon	sona
sorrel	docce
sought	sohtest
soul	hyge, saul, saule, sawle
soul-hoard	feorhhord
souls	sawla
souls (Latin)	animæ
sound	rædfest
south	suð
south-porch	suðportice
speak	cweðan
spirit	ferðe, gast, gastae, gastæ, gaste, modsefan
splendid	freolice
spoke	gyddode, hleoðrode, maðelode
spoken	gesæd
sprout	crop
Stamford	Stanford
stands	standeð
steeple	styple
steps	steppa
still	gyt
stolen	forstolen, stolenne
stones	stanas
stood	stode
storms	scurum
strawberry	streawbergean
strength (Latin)	fortis
strengths	mægen
strong	stronge
strong souled	modhwatu
subjected	nyde
successful	sigisiþa
such	hwylce, swylce
such as	swylce
suddenly	lungre
supplicant (Latin)	supplex

Old English Charms, Poems, and Proverbs 1   Word List (English to Ænglisc)

English	Ænglisc
support	fylste, geoce, gioce
surely	huru
surged	scyndeð
surrounded	biþeaht, biworpen
swarming	swirman
swept-away	fornam
sword	billum, mece, mecum, swurde
sword-play	sweordplegan
sword-wounded	sweordwund
swore	swor

T, t

English	Ænglisc
take	feta, fo, fone, nim, niman
taken	genam
tears-apart	tosliteð
teary	tearige
tell	saga, secgan
temptation	costunga
ten	tyn
than	ðon, þan, þonne
thane	ðegen
thank	geþancie, þance
that	ða, ðær, ðæt, ðam, ðe, ðy, þa, þæm, þæs, þæt, þætte, þam, þe, þet, þon
that are	is
the	ða, ðaem, ðæm, ðam, ðan, ðe, ðene, ði, hi, him, se, seo, þa, þaem, þæne, þæs, þæt, þam, þam, þan, þe, þone
the Angles	englum
the best	betest
the book (Latin)	biblos
the Britons	bryttum
the country	edygled
the cross	crucem, Crux
the cross (Latin)	crux
the Danes	dena
the day	dæg
the dear	deore

English	Ænglisc
The Dore	Dor
the dwarf's	dweores
the eagle's	earnes
the earth	eorðan, eorþan
the east	oriente
the east (Latin)	oriente
the end	finit
the hallows	halewæge
the heavens	rodores
the host	rimde
the innocent	bealuleas
the island	ige
the king	kingc
the king (Latin)	regem
the Lord	drihten, dryhtne
the middle	midd
the name	noma
the north (Latin)	aquilone
the pain	dolh
the people	folces, leodum
the prince	þeodne
the proud	wlance
the ruling king	þrymcyningc
the saints (Latin)	sancti
the Saxons	sexum
the Scots	scottum
the south	meridie
the south (Latin)	austro
the throne	thronum
the virgin (Latin)	uirginem
the Wear	weor
the Welsh	walum
the west	occidente
the west (Latin)	occidente
the wolf's	wolues
the woods	wuda
the world	cosmo, worulda
the world (Latin)	mundum, orbem
the world's (Latin)	mundi
the wound	benne
the young	geong
the-birth	gebyrdtide
the-chamber	in
the-creator	metod
the-Creator, the-Creator	metode

Old English Charms, Poems, and Proverbs 1

English	Ænglisc
the-Danes	Dene
their	hyra
the-king's	cinges
the-lord	dryhten, dryhtne, þeoden
them	þam
the-measurer's	meotodes, metudæs
then	ða, ðonne, tha, þa, þænne, þam, þe, þon, þone, þonne
thenceforth	siþþan
Theodric	ðeodric
the-other	oþre
there	ðær, ðære, ðer, þær, þar, þer, þonne
therefore	ðy, þi
these	ðem, ðes, hire, þas
the-wall	weal
the-world	worulde
they	ðem, hi, hine, hy, sunt, þæm
they are	sindon
they-are (Latin)	sunt
thing	þinga
think	gehicgenne, þence, wene
thirty	xxx
this	ðæs, ðas, ðeos, ðere, ðes, ðis, ðisse, hit, þæs, þas, þeos, þis, þison, þyos
this wound	benne
thistle	þystel
those	ðara, þone, þonne
though	ðeah, þe, þeah, þeh
thought	ðohte, geþohte, þances
thoughts	gemind
thought-wiser	ðonosnottorra, þoncsnotturra
thousand	ðusend
three	þry, þrym
three times	þriwa
three-times	III, þriwa
thrive	geþeoh
throb	hoppettan
thrones	throno

Word List (English to Ænglisc)

English	Ænglisc
through	ðurh, þurh
throw	forweorp
throw down	oferweorp
Thureth	þureð
thus	ðus, swa, þus
ties	teage
time	tid, tiid
titled	teode, tiadæ
to	ðe, to
to be	wæs
to kill	aþecgan
to look	locian
to me	me
to send	onsendon
to the	þære
to us	us
to Widia	widian
to Wulf (a name)	wulfes
to you	þine
to-be	siae, sie, sy
together	geador, gemonge, gesomnad
to-him	him
told	secgan
to-mark	gemearcian
tongue	tungan
too	eac, to
took	genom, namon
top-of-the-head	moldan
to-seek	secan
to-thee	ðe
toward	toward
town	burh, buruh, byrig
to-you	ðe
trappings	geatwum
treasure	maðma
treasures	madma
trees	treowum
trembling	byfigynde
troops	weorudes
true	
truly	huru, soð
trusted-friends	treowgeþofta
trusts	gelifeð
truth-fastened	soðfæsta, soðfæstan
truth-firm	soðfæst

Old English Charms, Poems, and Proverbs 1 — Word List (English to Ænglisc)

English	Ænglisc		English	Ænglisc
turn	gecyrre, hweorfað, hworfan		ward	uard, weard
twenty	twentig, xx		warfare	wigrædenne
twenty four	xxiiii		warrior	ordwyga, secg, wiga
twenty-eight	xxviii		warriors	oretmægcum, wiggendra
two-things	twega		was	wære, wæs, wes
			was hidden	abscondita

U, u

			was-not	ne
under	under		waste-away	weornie, weornige
undertake	ongunn		water	wætre, weter
undertaking	gahwem		water elf disease	wæterælfadle
undertook	ongan		wave	yþ
universal	gemæne		waves	brymmas, yðum
unknowing	uncuþ		waxed	weox
unlike	ungelic, ungelice		waypoint	ætstealle
unnumbered	unarimeda		we	we
unrelated	unmægas		wealth	welan, weolan
un-right	unriht, unryhte		weapon	hildefrofre
until	oðþæt, oþ		weather	weder
upon us	us		weight (Latin)	pondus
us	us, usic, ussum		Weland's	welandes
			Weland's (name)	Welande
			well	wel

V, v

			wellbeing	godes
valour	dryhtscipe		welling	weallendan
various-ways	mislice		well-known	gecyðed
very-much	swiðe		wen	wenne
vessel	hordfate		were	wæran, wære, wæron
vestment	reaf		west	west
victories	sigora		west-end	westende
victorious-women	sigewif		wet	bestemed
victory	sige		what	hwæt
virtue	duguðe		what-of	huaet, hwæt, hwet
virtue (Latin)	uirtute		when	ðonne, þa, þonne
voice (Latin)	uoce		whenever	þonne
			whereby	þonne
			which	ðe, hwilcne, þe

W, w

			which (Latin)	que
			while	hwile
			white	hwit
			Whitwell Gap	Hwitanwyllesgeat
wafer	oflætan		who	ðe, hwa, se, þe
wafers	oflætan		who (Latin)	quem, qui
Waldere	waldere		wide	rumre, widan, wide
walking	gangan		widely	wide
			Widia	widia

123

Old English Charms, Poems, and Proverbs 1 — Word List (English to Ænglisc)

English	Ænglisc
wielded	wealdan
wild	wilda, wilde
will	willa, willað
will (Latin)	uoluntate
will-be	wiorðeð, wiurðit, wyrþeþ
willing	wile
will-not	ne
Winchester (place)	Wincestre
wing	ueþer
winters	wintra
winters-numbered	wintergeteles
wise	froda
wiser	snotera
wished	wolde
wishes	wyle
with	mid, midd
with (Latin)	cum
with them	heom
wither away	geweornie
withers	onbere
within	binnan, innan
without	butan
wonder	uundra, wundra
wondrous	wuldres, wundorlicne, wundrum
wondrously	wundrum
wood	wudu
wood-fastened	wudafæstern
word	word, worde
words	wordum
word-vows	wordbeot
work	labor, weorcum, worc
work (Latin)	ponus
work-of	uerc, weorc
works	gehwylcre
world	gesceaft, woruld
world-kingdom	woruldrice
wormwood	wermod
worst	wyrrestan, wyrstan
worth	wurðe
worthiness	weorða, wurðlice
worth-minded	weorðmynda
worthship	weorþscipe
worthy	wearð, wyrðe
wound	wund

English	Ænglisc
wounds	wunde
wrathfully	wraþe
write	writan
writer of books	bocera
writings	gewritu, writ
wrote	awrat
Wulf (a name)	wulf

Y, y

English	Ænglisc
yet	ðeah, gen, gy, þa
yew berry	eowberge
you	ðe, ðin, ðu, eow, ge, þe, þu
young and brave	hagestealde
your	ði, ðin, ðinne, þin, þine, þinne, þinre, þinum
yours	þinre, þinum
yourself	selfne
youth	gecheðe
youth's	geonges

www.ingramcontent.com/pod-product-compliance
Lightning Source LLC
Chambersburg PA
CBHW051418070526
44584CB00023B/3475